To Gen

MW01614318

Brown Skin and the Brilliant Sun

A Poet's Opus

Terry E. Carter

By Terry E. Carter

Terésa J. Carter, Editorial Consultant

Blessings!

Brown Skin
and the
Brilliant Sun
A Poet's Opus

Terry E. Carter

Xulon Press
555 Winderley Pl, Suite 225
Maitland, FL 32751
407.339.4217
www.xulonpress.com

© 2023 by Terry E. Carter

All rights reserved solely by the author. The author guarantees all contents are original and do not infringe upon the legal rights of any other person or work. No part of this book may be reproduced in any form without the permission of the author. The views expressed in this book are not necessarily those of the publisher.

Unless otherwise indicated,Scripture quotations taken from the Holy Bible, New International Version (NIV). Copyright © 1973, 1978, 1984, 2011 by Zondervan.

Used by permission. All rights reserved.
Paperback ISBN-13: 978-1-66288-529-7
Ebook ISBN-13: 978-1-66288-530-3

--Foreword--

"To North, to East, to South, to West
Thy loyal children make their way.
To execute thy fine behest,
Go turn the darkness into day!"

(— John W. Work, Sr., *The Gold and Blue*,
Fisk University Alma Mater)

With this, his sixth volume of poetry, appropriately named "Brown Skin and the Brilliant Sun...", Brother Terry E. Carter has once again answered the clarion call of the third stanza of Fisk University's alma mater by illuminating shaded corners of eager, or not so eager minds with his brilliantly lyrical, thought provoking, challenging, but oh so entertaining, (dare I say head bobbing, foot tapping) rhythmic prose. Mr. Carter has the uncanny ability to meter his words to synchronize with our internal diaspora-crossing metronomes. And that syncopated collaboration between author and reader, is the reason we sometimes "feel" his words, even before we start to really hear them.

I first met Terry "TC" Carter, on those glorious, historic forty acres of Fisk University's campus in 1978-79, when I was a Freshman, and he was an upperclassman in his Junior year. The campus was teeming with exuberant, brilliant young minds, well aware that they were not just figuratively, but literally walking in WEB DuBois' footsteps.

Many considered themselves future members of his vaunted "Talented Tenth". Yet even in that environment, in those hallowed halls, there were those who stood above the rest. Terry Carter stood tall and his name rang out. He was well on his way to graduating Summa Cum Laude, and earning a Phi Beta Kappa key (both of which he did), and we could all see his trajectory was destined for that rarefied air that most would not experience.

Beyond this, the brother had the gift of being able to spontaneously articulate his thoughts in a manner that just sounded, (in the vernacular of the day), "smooth". You wanted to hear Terry speak. He was one of those people of whom you always thought: "I could listen to him all day", instead of "I feel as though he's been talking all day!" I sometimes tried to speak to others using the same phrase or phrases that Terry had used to speak to me. I had all the right words, but I (we all), lacked the natural lyricism and rhythm that Terry demonstrated then, and his poetry demonstrates now.

And this is why it comes as no surprise, that Terry E. Carter, Christian, Husband, Father, Friend Fiskite, Author and Poet Laureate, has now penned six volumes of very well-received and acclaimed poetry in "The Brown-Skinned" series. Dear Reader, I do hope you will avail yourselves of the wisdom in the following pages. Read and listen, not just with your eyes and ears, but feel and experience with your hearts and souls. And when you suddenly realize that your head is bobbing, and your feet are tapping, you will truly be experiencing not just "Brown Skin and the Brilliant Sun", but also, The Brown Skinned Poet, our BRILLIANT Son!

Reginald D. Jackson, Fisk '82
"Her Sons and her Daughters are ever on the altar."

--Dedications/ Acknowledgments/ Thanks--

This book is the end product of an agonizing and energizing period in my life. While I haven't intentionally suffered for my art, I've witnessed a lot of suffering around me and been stung by it on occasion myself. COVID-19 has been an aggressive and persistent reality in all of our lives. So I've paid some attention to this pandemic poetically. Re-emerging racism and white supremacy has been a dangerous and alarming reality in all of our lives. So I've paid considerable attention to this danger poetically. Allyship, faith, hope, and love have been consistent buoys on the hazardous waters of all of our lives, so I've delighted in recognizing these life preservers poetically.

As I approach three full years as a cancer survivor, I dedicate this "opus" of my literary work to my father Varnie, my mother Jean, and my baby brother Scott. I know that they're still watching over me from heavenly places and I curse cancer every day for physically taking them all away.

This book is also dedicated to my first "stomping ground". Medford, MA is both the city of my birth and the place where my personal poetic journey began. In 2021, Medford recognized this journey by conferring upon me the city's inaugural title of Poet Laureate. My two-year term just ended, but the impact of that honor is really just beginning. For Medford, and particularly for my homefolk in the Ville (West Medford)...I'm honored and I'm on it!

Finally, I want to thank everyone who participated at whatever level in the GoFundMe artist's campaign that has underwritten the publication of the "Brilliant Sun". Admittedly, your faith and support should have resulted in a more prudent result. Still, the old adage must apply, "what's worth having is worth waiting for." The wait is over. Welcome to another *Brilliant Sun(rise)*.

I hope that you can revel in the jazz of this thing...the pizzazz of this thing...the razzmatazz of this thing!

That's my story and I'm sticking to it.

May the Lord God make His face to shine upon you.

T.E.C.
Summer, 2023

--Contents--

--Motion-- 255

--My Truth--

"Let your eyes be offended by the sight of lying and deceitful men."

Hopi Proverb

A Letter to the Man I Used to Be

I was once afraid of my own shadow...
timid, hesitant, easily shook.
They say that pressure bursts pipes.
My spiritual plumbing was shot.
My mental mechanics needed overhauling.
My soul's electrical wiring was shorting out.
My works closet didn't have a prayer.

You're looking at me
with a mixed countenance
of surprise and bewilderment,
almost as if you've forgotten
the way things used to be.
Preacher says he gives the same message
over and over again,
because he knows
the Saints leak.

He must be right.
'Cause you ought to remember
the not-so-good days,
the not-so-great nights,
the fraught weeks,
and the funky years.
You just ought to remember.

Still...if a brother stays
at the table long enough,
he might get dealt a
a winning hand or two.
The acne and the awkwardness didn't last.
Confidence came on me fast.
Some pretty girls forgot my past.
The swagger made this bust a blast.

Yes, I'm checking you out...
The sisters might say,
"He's got it goin' on."
Big job, big house, big money,
fly whip, boat slip,
and a honey on his hip
at all times.
He might not be Mr. Right,
but he darn sure is Mr. Right Now.

I went in on the weekend.
Poppin' bub at the club...
Gettin' play right away...
Thursday night thrills,
Friday night lights and
Saturday Night Fever.
No remorse, no regrets...
Hell, I barely remember most of it.

Almost got tagged with some
baby mama drama...
some Billie Jean junk.
Sister tried to float some bunk.
But surprisingly (at least to me)...
the real pops showed up
and showed proof.
The kid was not my son.

Still, it's not the stuff of poetry.
And I'm writing this letter
so you can see,
I wasn't the man
God called me to be.
I was the joker and the jerk.
I tried to be woke, without the work.
Not the purpose, just the perk...
most of the duty I'd sooner shirk.

Still...if a brother gets up
from the table to stretch...
he might get a sense,
that's he's just been a wretch.
He just might see a roughed-out sketch.
Amazing grace might let him catch
all the bad apples in his batch.
Skin deep beauties never match,
just gold diggers trying to latch,
onto the man I used to be.

Now that I have the revelation,
I want to reveal my whole situation.
I want to pass on the explanation,
and enter in to the new creation,
God has put in play for me.

So if you're reading this sinner's letter,
please know that I want to do better...
to release my bonds and soul unfetter,
as a new kind of faith-filled true trend-setter,
not the old man who'd become an abettor,
now the lender, who's no more a debtor.

Yes, if you've gotten this heartfelt note,
know that I'm putting on Joseph's coat,
embracing this life of many hues...
shedding my layers of sin and blues.
Declaring intentions to let God use
a life that I surely tried to abuse,
and one that I easily stood to lose.

This is a letter to the man I used to be.
The brother writing is the one that God set free.
Yet I have no delusions 'bout my soul's infirmity.
A work in progress...that's all I'll ever claim to be.

Black Seeds

Part of the problem
is that many of you
can only take this Black thing
in very small doses.
You don't want no protestin'
no addressin' and no investin'...
You need that Aunt Jemima Black,
that Uncle Ben's Black,
that Stepin Fetchit Black,
that Clarence Thomas Black,
that Booker T. Black,
that in denial Black...
versus that unapologetically Black.

You kinda' thrown
by that Nina Simone Black,
by that James Baldwin Black,
by that Muhammad Ali Black,
by that Dubois and Robeson Black,
by that Toni Morrison Black,
by that Angela Davis Black,
by that Huey P. Newton Black,
by that Malcolm X Black,
by that Public Enemy Black,
by that John Carlos, Tommie Smith and Colin Kaepernick Black,
by that straight ghetto Black,
by that self-lovin' Black,
by that slaves that fought back Black,
by that y'all can kiss my butt Black.

We not livin' in the politically correct right now.
We not drivin' on the safe side of diversity, equity and inclusion.
This ain't about humility and assimilation.

This ain't about wholesale incarceration.
This ain't about making' folks feel comfortable.
We not claimin' that people of color posturing.
We steppin' into the danger waters.
We talkin' by Black, for Black, be Black...
Black music, unadulterated,
Black literature, unexpurgated,
Black art, un-eviscerated,
Black love, un-emasculated,
Black thought, un-eradicated.

Love me some Diahann Carroll;
but this ain't the Julia season.
Love me some Claire Huxtable;
but this ain't the Cosby Show season.
Love me some Johnny Mathis;
but this ain't the wonderful, wonderful season.
Love me some Tiger Woods;
but this ain't no country club season.
Love me some Ray Charles;
but this ain't no "America The Beautiful" season.
Love me some Paul Laurence Dunbar;
but this ain't no cabin and field season.

The worst of your kind
has got it in for
the best of our kind...
for our women,
for our children,
for our history,
and our legacy,
for our accomplishments,
for our neighborhoods,
and our villages,
and our faith,
and our truth.

You can grudgingly admire
the superstars,
the prize-winners,
the great entertainers,
the champions,
the high achievers,
the big earners,
and the brand names...
until the unforgivable blackness
rears its ugly head.

Then hate drowns out the love
for Oprah,
for Lebron,
for Spike,
for Denzel,
for Jim Brown,
and Serena and Venus,
for Chuck D. and Tupac,
for Barack and Michelle,
for Marvin Gaye,
and MLK.

You wanna' ban real blackness...
real Black books,
real Black heroes,
real Black role models,
real Black warriors,
real Black kings,
and real Black queens.
You trying to bury us
without realizing,
that all you're doing is planting seeds...
and like the Main Ingredient sang
back in the day:

"Listen to the story the drums tell...
 Black seeds keep on growing!"

 Critical Race Theory explains it well...
"Black seeds keep on growing!"

 You shrug your shoulders and scream, "what the hell..."
"Black seeds keep on growing!"

 Pavlov would instruct you, just listen to the bell...
"Black seeds keep on growing!"

A Mama's Boy Too...

I've always seen my daddy's face,
when I look in a mirror,
through a clear windowpane,
or at "selfie" time
on my I-phone.

Always my daddy's face...

The strength of his chin.
The cut of his jaw.
The resolution in his eyes.
The jolly laughter in his cheeks.

Yet in these Covid-cast, Zoom communities
we now to gather in,
I've seen my Mama's face
looking back at me,
in the rectangle
labeled Terry C.

Her knowing gaze.
Her reflective glance.
Her softly furrowed brow.
Her Mona Lisa smile.

To tell the whole truth,
I was a bit conflicted
about the whole Zoom thing—
Yet another bunch of meetings,
that I dreaded having to attend.

But I know I owe
that little digital rectangle
a debt of gratitude today.

I have longed for ages to see
the knowing gaze,
the reflective glance,
the softly furrowed brow,
and the Mona Lisa smile...
on my own,
more than mature face.

Lord knows I love my daddy.
I've always loved his strong chin,
his chiseled jaw,
his resolute eyes,
and the jolly laughter in his cheeks.

But I've always considered myself
a Mama's boy too...
patient, kind, compassionate,
and resourceful—
in a different way.

Now the burden of proof,
doesn't weigh me down so heavily.
The sense of longing has subsided.
In the little rectangle
labeled Terry C.,
I see my Mama looking back at me too...

And my soul is satisfied.

Brown Skin and the Brilliant Sun

To have this sprinkle of melanin,
that gives an umber to Negro skin
and codifies the African,
the native, or some Latin kin...

I treasure all this represents.
Though some may feel it gives offense,
and still not wish to widen tents,
that bring about fair recompense.

My opus and evolving story
binds to Afro-centric glory,
yielding tales of righteous pride,
moving hatred to the side.

Still the same and wondrous sun,
cures the frame that I have won.
Some might call me sepia-toned,
high-yellow, or perhaps red-boned.

I claim the black and brown and tan,
my legacy and who I am,
baked beneath the golden orb,
that yields the brilliance I absorb.

Without Works

I'm not saying don't pray.
The Lord hears your petitions
for peace and safety and sobriety.
The Lord sees your bended knees.
He understands your anguish
and will comfort you...

But He also sees the zealotry
and flawed logic
of the ones who cry
my freedoms,
my rights,
the Constitution.

He sees the foul report
of the NRA behemoth,
and pocketed politicians,
and the MAGA-mutinous.

He sees the hardened heart,
and the unsympathetic spirit,
and the corrupted character,
and the violent intent.

He has ordained that faith
without works is as dead
as the 19 in Uvalde,
the 14 in Buffalo,
the 58 in Vegas,
the 49 in Orlando,
the 32 in Blacksburg,
the 27 in Newtown,
the 26 in Sutherland Springs,

the 23 in Killeen,
the 23 in El Paso,
and the 9 in Charleston.

Those dead are in His eternal keeping.
More dead are in our will and manifest.

How much longer will we agonize,
but not act.
How much longer will we wring our hands,
but not change.
How much longer will we keep machinery in play
that kills our children everyday...
every single day.
How much longer will we let the godlessness of a few
bring doom and dread and death
into the living rooms, schools, and sanctuaries
of the beloved community.

I'm not saying don't pray.
But we will never have real peace,
without real justice
and genuine accountability.
If we allow it to forever be
all about the banks,
and the stocks,
and the free market,
and the bottom line...
that's what it's always going to be about.

If we let them continue to talk us, bend us,
and buy us out of doing what is right,
they will always be empowered
to do what is patently wrong,
always be influenced to do
what is painfully abusive,

always be paid and pay-rolled
to do what is poison and perverse.

120+ guns per civilian
in this country...
and that's just the ones
we think we know about.
Is there an ounce of sanity
in that equation?
Is that not a perfect storm
for the emotionally unstable,
for the mentally unbalanced,
for the violently predisposed,
for the harbingers of hatred,
and for the power of suggestion
over the ignorant and unhinged.

I'm not saying don't pray.
I'm getting off my knees right now.
But this time,
I've asked God
to give me the courage
to do more,
and do differently,
and be the change
I want to see in this nation.

I've asked Him to compel us
to join our mustard seeds together,
and sow our kernels of faith
in strength and unity,
to move this mountain
of violence and murder
to distant, forbidden shores...
beyond our sadness and our sense of loss,
beyond our living rooms, our schools, and our sanctuaries,

beyond our beloved community,
beyond the malls, motels, offices,
meeting halls, parks, and playgrounds...
and beyond the sheltering spaces
we call home.

Kill the Poets First

Kill the poets first...
for they will tell the truth
and shame the devil
in all of us.
They will highlight
the lack of honor among thieves
with assonance, alliteration
and clever metaphor.

Put them in shackles
and parade them through the public square.
Strip them naked,
if you dare.
They will expose
the libertarian as the libertine,
amid the piles of gluttony,
hubris, pride, and prejudice
that lie at his gout-ridden feet.

They will rightly divide the gospel
in ways that the jack-leg,
and the profligate, and the
snake-oil purveyor
conflate, confuse, and contradict
at every pulpit and podium.

They will measure with meter
the length of the bigot's bloodline,
the strength of the captor's confine,
the mark of the beastly revenant,
the lies which prove most fraudulent,
the truth that men seek to circumvent.

Kill the poets first.
For their lyrics,
like fine opera,
will peel away the lie,
and pare down the malice,
and point out the mayhem
in rhyming couplets,
and piquant haiku,
and epic odes,
and hip-hop for the homeboys.

With their "black lives matter"
and their "save the planet",
and their "no justice, no peace",
they will roll the bedrocks
of the right wing,
of the rabid racist,
and the reluctant witness
back down the mountain we've scaled,
like a Sisyphus stone...
over and over and over,
again.

Kill the poets first...
by the bullet and the ballot,
by the garrot and the glock and the guillotine and the gas chamber,
by a thousand disappearing acts and a hundred hidden dungeons,
by the noose, from the bough of an ancient oak...
That is the ultimate attention getter,
a foolproof message sender,
greater in gore than any artist can render,
crucifixion for the commoner
and the crusader.

Owe no allegiance to the song.
Vow not to the charming verses.

Smile not at the fragrant lyric.
Hide not the pretty sonnet
in the bowels of
your heart of darkness...

Kill them first.

They will trick you.
You will feel the pangs
of your lost humanity
welling up in your bosom.

They will convict you,
make you want to buy back your soul
from long-departed demons
who made you crave sin.

They will be the straw
that breaks your camel's loyal back
and causes your beast of burden
to spurn the desert of your depravity.

Don't let them hold a mirror to your faces.
Don't let their light shine on shameful places.
Don't let them put your hounds through their paces.
Don't let their judges handle your cases.

Kill the poets.
Kill the poets.
Kill the poets first.

More Than Just Magic

Don't y'all be mad...
I know it's the current fad.
But I can't bring myself to call it
Black Girl Magic.
It's not near enough explanation,
for this degree of transformation.

Yes, y'all make the miraculous
look minimal.
But it's not abracadabra easy,
none of it.
Raising three kids without a daddy
and makin' a Section 8 say welcome home,
ain't that easy.

Holding down three jobs
to keep the lights on,
keep food in the fridge,
keep the gas tank full,
and pay off a mountain
of student loans,
ain't that easy.

Being around haters, gossipers,
crabs in a barrel,
and back-biters all day...
and not gettin' any on ya',
ain't that easy.

Raising rose bushes in city dirt
with a country smile...
with a Navy brat's wanderlust
and a southern belle's style,
ain't that easy.

Full-on Maybelline pretty,
a no MAC, no-crack complexion,
without a stitch of
foundation, blush, eye-liner, fake lashes
and two shades of lip gloss...
ain't that easy.

Climbing to the to the top
of a corporate ladder,
with the white boys all around you
steady getting madder,
ain't that easy.

There's not a Harry Potter wand,
or a Ruby Slipper click,
or a Dr. Strange spell
in the world,
that can do what you do,
with Wakanda wishes
and Harlem River Drive dreams.

Yes, y'all make the miraculous
look minimal.
But it's not abracadabra easy,
none of it.

It's not as simple as Shazam.
It's not a clever sleight of hand.
It's not prestidigitation,
or a genie situation.

So let's get up off of
the Black Girl Magic stuff.
I'm pretty well convinced,
that won't nearly be enough.

No, won't nearly be enough,
to describe what's happenin' here...
when a sister's on her game,
and the men bring up the rear.

No, Seriously...

This aging stuff is real;
and it ain't necessarily graceful either...
Stuff be cracking and creaking...
Sitting, standing, reeking,
painful lessons it is leaking.

It's not pretty.
I make snorts, cackles, grunts and sighs...
so often, that it mortifies,
my thirty-year-old sensibilities
of the brother I think I'm s'posed to be.

Oh noble youth...
wherefore art thou?
Sagacity and veracity and tenacity seem so overrated,
when what you long for is agility and virility,
and some distance from senility.

I can remember roller-skating at the Bal-a-Roue
in nineteen hundred and seventy-two.
But now I don't know where my glasses are,
when they're sitting right on top of my head.
Why did I even get out of bed?
Oh yeah, I had to go pee.
Shouldn't have had that last cup of tea.
My continence ain't what it used to be.

This aging stuff is real.
Gettin' that check from the government,
Social Security payin' my rent.
Won't ever get back all the money I lent.
Don't even matter,
it's already spent.

So many things on my bucket list...
a lot of fine ladies I never kissed.
A Rolex has never adorned my wrist.
And the mega-millions...I guess I just missed.
Promises, promises...you get the gist!

No, seriously...
a thousand journeys to distant lands,
sinking my toes in paradise sands,
backstage passes from my favorite bands...
just let it go bro'.
It's out of your hands.

Perhaps I'll see that 50th reunion,
or seventy-five years of taking communion.
My folks were married for sixty-plus.
At just thirty-five, can I make any fuss?
Retirement beckons...so does rust!

So many friends are
dead and gone.
I cried for them all,
but I had to move on.
Stings quite a bit,
but what can you do,
'cept thank the Lord
that He didn't call you.

Over There, Over Here

They didn't go fight over there,
so you could burn down their homes,
and lynch their young boys,
and lust after their young girls,
and terrorize their families...
over here.

They didn't go bleed over there,
so you could keep their communities poor,
and make them labor in menial jobs,
and force them to work your fields,
and take half of every penny they earned...
over here.

They didn't go die over there,
so you could redline their neighborhoods,
and refuse them fair credit,
and deny them due process,
and mis-educate their children...
over here.

They didn't go over there,
so you could deny their GI claims,
and cheat their beneficiaries,
and disrespect their uniforms,
and denigrate the valor of their service...
over here.

They didn't go over there
and march as Buffalo Soldiers,
and grind as Harlem Hellfighters,
and soar as Tuskegee Airmen,
so you could hide them from your history books...
over here.

They didn't go over there
and languish in POW camps,
and be tortured by foreign hosts,
and suffer from profound and permanent trauma,
so you could trample on their civil liberties...
over here.

They went over there
and carried the flag into battle,
and crusaded for a cause,
and defended a way of life,
so you could hold to self-evident truths...
over here.

They went over there
and showed extraordinary courage,
and created a heroic legacy,
and garnered the respect of their foes,
so that you could enjoy inalienable rights...
over here.

They went over there
and embraced the call to serve,
and gave their lives in honor,
and never denied their nation's face,
so that you could be proud Americans...
over here.

They went over there
and chased down angry despots,
and stared down determined killers,
and paid the ultimate price,
so that you could go to the baseball game,
and the green grocers, and the church bazaar in peace...
over here.

They went over there
and rose to every challenge,
and beat back every opponent,
and dedicated their lives to God and country,
so that you could honor their memory rightly...
over here.

Honor their memory rightly...
over here.

We, the People

These stripes are not a freak of nature.
There's nothing wrong with us.
Contrary to snide innuendo
and idle speculation,
and vicious gossip...
We're not the products of short circuits,
bad karma, demonic possession,
theatrical contrivance, comic book mutations,
or mischievous gods at play.

We are sons, daughters, brothers, sisters,
mother, fathers, friends and familiars.
We are kindred and connected,
even while we are estranged and excluded.
We are the forgotten invitation
and the difficult explanation.
We are the careless whispers
and the butt of the bad joke.

We are not prideful in ways
that make us mean and belligerent.
We are proud, in ways
that make us embrace the ones that are different,
and respect the ones that are the same.
We sign up first when allies are needed.
The call to arms we've always heeded.
We never shrink from the nation's duty.
We just want the nation to see our beauty.

Molded from universal clay,
here's most of what we came to say.

Today, we are bespoke.
We are the gift that keeps on giving,
despite the closets of our forebears,
the carefully cultivated lies of our kin,
the laws that would discard our reality,
and the labels society has glued to our eyelids.

Today we are authentic,
as real as a Rolex from Shreve, Crump and Low.
Today we are flawless,
like a perfect cut, IF grade, five carat Botswana solitaire.
Today we are genuine,
like Perrier and Poland Springs,
like a Verdi aria that Leontyne sings,
like a rose petal on which a dewdrop clings.

We have found beautiful voices.
We have created art beyond imagination.
We have made the stage and screen
bear witness to the rising tide.
We have danced with deities and dragons,
and lived to tell the tales of new miracles.

We are active and alive today,
beyond epidemic and persecution and exclusion.
We are dynamic and undeniable,
in spite of the silent assassins and the angry zealots.
We are poetic and powerful...
and like the old Gospel song calls out,
we shall not be moved.

We have nursed the sick
and raised the babies.
We have marched for causes
and colors and choices.
We have taught in schools

and untangled history's lies.
We have built businesses
and fostered American dreams.
We shall not be moved.

We have protested and prayed and paraded.
We have been bloodied and beaten.
We have been dismissed and disrespected.
We have been shocked and shuttered.
We have been labeled and limited.
We have been maligned, mistreated, and misunderstood.
But... we shall not be moved.

Don't be mad at God today, or ever.
He doesn't make mistakes.
She doesn't make mistakes.
They don't make mistakes.
The universe isn't going to collapse
under the weight of our planks, our platforms, or our politics.
The tent's big enough, people...
big enough for your people, my people, our people
and we the people.

We're not a plague, or a virus, or a disease.
No matter who you cut,
the same blood runs warm and red.
The same things that kill you and your loved ones,
kill us and the folks we love too.
Gay is still a lovely word,
and can be freely used
to express feelings of cheerfulness, merriment,
and lighthearted excitement.

You may never pay allegiance to this rainbow flag.
But the banner over all of us is love.
And we choose to love

in every flavor that nature makes.
These stripes are not contrived or conjured up.
They are the greater gifts of our pride,
perhaps to be distilled, but never to be denied.
And you can look away if you want to.
When you look back,
we'll still be standing right here.
We're not hiding today.
We're not hiding tomorrow.
We're not hiding, ever again.

In honor of Medford (MA) Pride Month,
June, 2022

Tolerance Ain't Easy

We love our babies too...
We don't teach them to cheat and lie.
We don't raise them to kill or die.

We thought they'd have hope and a future.
We sacrificed and struggled and bled
to ease the way.

We prayed unceasingly.
We were on our knees crying out,
to God be the glory.

And still...

We're watching history repeat itself.
We're bleeding again in the streets.
We're watching our babies get targeted, beat, and slain.
We're watching our mothers wail and scream.

We cry for every candle of hope that blows out.
We cry for every promising future that fades to black.
We cry for every good seed that can't find good soil to grow in.

Then we gather our souls for strength.
We put on the full armor of God anew.
We hitch our courage to the sticking post.
We march, we shout out, and we stand.

God will not be mocked.

So we wrestle with demons of hate and segregation's ghosts.
We wrestle with modern-day lynchings...
and the growing hubris of our former captors.
We wrestle with modern-day masters
who wish to enslave us yet again.

We have so much more to do.
But we are still here...
and the work continues...

We convene to have dialogue.
We break bread together.
We meditate and mourn.
We strategize and formulate.
We'll read and write and publish and protest.
We're persistent and progressive and purpose-driven.
We're beating the different drums,
and lighting those candles
that curse the darkness.

We won't make it simple for them...
the ones that want us to dissolve,
and despair,
and disperse,
and disappear.

We'll rebuild what they destroy.
We'll reclaim what they reproach.
We'll restore what they remove.
We'll revere what they revile.

We'll listen to our righteous leaders.
When they go low,
we'll go high.
We'll revel in
the audacity of hope.
We'll shelter, and shield,
and cover, and collaborate.
We'll survive and advance
We'll live to fight another day...
by any means necessary.

We will train up our children
in the way they should go.
We will teach them the hard lessons
of history's true course
and the daily task of vigilance.
They will be wide awake
with the wisdom of legacy,
and the fruit of the spirit.
They will love their neighbors...
and lift up their allies.
They will seek reconciliation.
They will embrace the rainbow
and invite the different ones in.
They will take the road less traveled,
and show us courage under fire.

We have so much more to do.
But we are still here...
and the work continues...

Tolerance ain't easy...

--Home--

"With all things and in all things, we are relatives."

Sioux Proverb

Let Medford Be a Blessing: An Inaugural Ode

You didn't come for a civics lesson,
or ask this poet to teach the session.
And yet, the bard is honor-bound
to spread this gospel all around.
To all who hear these words today,
I'm offering this winning play.
Beyond mere pomp and window dressing,
I say, let Medford be a blessing.

Politics as a contact sport—
that shouldn't be the last report.
Though we may scuffle like cats and dogs...
the wheel must spin with many cogs.
Forgiveness is a fruit of the spirit.
We must be able to grin and bear it.
This is the stuff of neighborhood.
We come together for common good.

Strident voices will raise alarm,
decrying the town's historic charm.
Let not dissension be the farm,
where anger sows the seeds of harm.
In new opinion and fresh insight,
we gain new vision to make things right.
Let's make the list and check it twice.
Respect for all will blend the spice.
Respect for the old, as well as the new...
Respect for the red, the white and the blue...
Respect for the tried, the tested, the true...
Respect for the path of your neighbor's shoe...

A divide and conquer mentality,
can never lead to community,
can never sponsor equality,
can never rejoice in diversity,
can never host creativity,
can never buy universality,
can never delight in veracity,
is never a righteous reality.

Let's meet where streams of hope converge,
and move beyond the spiteful urge.
That's not the road where we should merge.
It only leads the vain to purge.
It only fuels pandemic surge.

Let's be that bright and shining town,
where good folks gather from all around.
We don't build fences to keep folks out.
We don't fill our children with constant doubt.
Despite the season of Covid we're in,
we haven't let viral exposure win.
We've worn our masks and taken our shots.
We haven't come down with scales and green spots.

Within our fractured history,
remains a shroud of mystery.
And so we seek to bare the truth,
beyond our own confession booth.
We stand on shoulders of our best,
the ones who mastered every test,
Black and white and tan and brown,
who pushed to build this wondrous town.

We hold their stories close and dear.
They salt and seed our atmosphere,
tales of courage and wisdom abound,
which make our commons hallowed ground.

We battle against the enemy,
that looks to bring adversity,
that looks to turn our hearts away,
from kindred ties that rule the day.

Such is the call to a city's soul,
the road that leads to a common goal.
Such is the nature of clasping hands,
that move in concert, as faith demands.
We've overcome such pain and grief,
but tried to hold to our belief,
that standing at the edge of night,
is promise in God's perfect light.

We honor our heroes with tempered pride,
but never toss the struggling aside.
We recognized that rising tides,
lift the ships where freedom rides.
It's not parades that make us great.
It's making room for the lost and the late.
We build our legacy out of the past,
to godly acts we cling to fast,
to all four winds, the dross we cast,
remembering to lift the last.

How do we get to that promised place,
where all may share abundant grace?
How do we break down rough-hewn walls,
to reach that land where challenge falls?
What do our differences amplify?
How can diversity multiply,
the cultural soup we want to try,
the blended family's strong reply?

We sit and talk to make things right.
We work out issues in plain sight.

We build consensus, day and night.
We don't make war to show our might.
We share a meal to ease our fears.
We welcome folks with new ideas.
We find the laughter that always endears.
We offer shoulders to capture our tears.
We smile when human contact nears.

This is the strength of community,
where neighborhoods strive for dignity,
where diverse people share a bond,
that ignorance may frown upon.
This is the goal of the fair and the just,
to break down walls and build up trust.
Who can dispute such fellowship?
We cling now with this noble grip.
We'll work to ease our fear of strangers,
and not advance new trials or dangers.
We'll strive to make our city's crest,
always stand for Medford's best.
Here is our hand of strength extended.
We won't let friendship be upended.
All of our people must be protected.
No one here should feel neglected.

We vote to achieve our common goals.
We meet each other at the polls.
We don't make rules to eliminate.
We move real equity onto the slate.
We show respect and minimize doubt.
We flow from a wide and open spout.
Let leadership speak to a brave, new vision,
that answers to all without derision.
Let public officials carry the weight,
of promoting peace and reducing hate.

At the end of the day, we're all we have,
to bind our wounds with Gilead's salve.
And so we measure each sunrise,
as ample chance to strategize,
as ample chance to grow more wise,
as ample chance to empathize,
as ample chance to change the lies,
as ample chance to grow our ties.

Let us lift as we climb to greater heights,
and strive to eliminate petty fights.
Let us look to the heavens as God reveals,
the fortune that our strife conceals.
Our grasp propels extended reach.
Let's always endeavor to rightly teach.
Let's always practice what we preach.
Let's follow our leaders into the breach.
Let's see the line before we cross,
embrace the gain, and cut the loss.

Mine is a message of healing first,
the blessing that quenches every thirst.
Mine is a letter to Medford's soul,
preaching for a unified goal.
We've seen disease and rage provoke,
some ignorance as wisdom spoke.
Now is the season for love and peace,
to lose our hearts in faith's release.

Mine is a call to redemptive grace,
the flame that lights the darkest space.
Mine is a letter to Medford's spirit.
Listen closely...Can't you hear it?
Today begins a brand new race,
a starting line for each fresh face,
a relay baton for a caravan,
of Black and brown and white and tan.

Unity is our path to peace.
Agreement makes all conflict cease.
Equity hunts for love's release,
as kindness cooks a hearty feast.
Back away from anger and threats.
Rage can never repay our debts.
Bring together our fishing nets,
and gather the catch without regrets.

So now you've had the civics lesson.
The poet yet must ask the question.
For still, this bard is honor-bound,
to show good proof that words resound.
To all who heard this ode today—
we clasp our hands and yes we pray,
a single hope we're all confessing...
We shout, let Medford be a blessing.

We shout, let Medford be a blessing.

*Offered on the occasion of the 2nd inauguration
of Breanna Lungo-Koehn, as Mayor of Medford, MA
January 2, 2022*

Place, Race, and Remembrance

Lamenting the loss of my touchstones
and my high altars...
Ahhh...place, race, and remembrance.

The grade school where I learned to read and write
became a condo for the first wave of bedroom community occupants,
a co-op for the early adopters of IPO dividends and bio-tech
windfalls.
The place was where I first heard of JFK's assassination...
everybody was crying,
and we didn't even understand why.
We understand now.
Martin and Medgar and Malcolm
gave us the lesson,
but did it really take?

Ol' Henry's Little Store
has been gone for fifty years.
All the penny candy is in trendy boutiques now.
It's sold by the pound these days,
and dispensed from plexi-glass tubes...
High end jelly beans come in 100 flavors.
Weird tastes like popcorn and Pepsi-Cola,
cost a lot more than any penny...
a whole lot more.

I remember needing to be off the street
before the street lights came on...
We were all still doing fake karate,
actin' like Bruce Lee,
and playing run the bases,
near the corner of Holton and Monument Streets.
We had to keep an eye out for the Braxton dogs.

There weren't any pit bulls or Rottweilers yet,
but Butch was pretty ornery and he liked to bite folks.

If you'd done something cool,
or been at all remarkable,
you had a nick-name...
The roll call is still pretty long,
but the absent far outweigh the present.

We knew all of these cats...
Fruitman, Spud, 'Wood/Hollywood, Smidlap, Walk, Harv', Craze Lace/
Jordache/J.C., Tip, Bav, Puddin', T.C./Top Cat, Jr./Lindz, Brak, Spizz/
Sparrow, Wiz, Zoom, Burton, J-Willy, Whit', Walt, Fibes, Wolf, Wolfie,
Garg', Sputnik, Oak, Coke/Co-Co, Rog', Flash, Ice, Doc', Von Eric,
Gibb, Bullet, Jed, Jab, Butchie, Buddy, Spanky, Ike, AD, Nelly, Wing,
Monk, Snake, Lambie, Richie Rich, Hulk, Stutsy, Foot, Humpty, Rocky,
Merv', Turtle, Zeke, Pooka, B.A./Farm, Abu, Bruno, Bunky, Squirrel,
Stony, Baron, Skipper, Putney, Sonny, Ol' Henry, the General, Chinky,
Stony, Cainsy, O.G., Earl, Java, Little Charlie, Rabbit, Skooch, Turk,
Creek, Piper...

And that's just the brothers...
just the brothers.

The place where we were wed
is a different kind of sanctuary now...
The pews have become padded settees
in a glitz and glass lobby.
Sacred vows have been replaced,
by lawyers, lease agreements,
and HOA fees.
Realtors and developers
ran off the pastors, deacons, and elders...
bought off the next generation,
and the next,
and the next.
The choir loft is a coffee counter.
The parish is a dog park.

The temple is a Bohemian tea house.
Dim Sum through the front door,
Tapas through the back.

My touchstones and my high altars
are little more than fond memories,
and sad truths of loss and surrender.
Occasional reunions call out
to the scattered and departed.
Home-going celebrations
gather the long-gone and the still standing
for lamentations, testimonies,
collard greens and fried chicken communions.

We won't have this for too much longer.
Place, race, and remembrance
are more for picture books and archives,
than safe harbor and inheritance.
The cats with all those nicknames
will surely become footnotes
in a set of encyclopedias
that has become
every bit as obsolete
in this brave new world of
Siri, AI, Google and Amazon.

Song-poet sang of
"time re-writing every line."
My lyric is not a re-write.
We may not have a chance to do it all again.
So this is just me,
waiting for the last moves
on the Ville's chess board...
waiting for the brothers
to play that last game
at the park Col. Dugger built,

or the courts Cleedie Rhone built.
I am lamenting the loss of my touchstones
and my high altars...

Lamenting the loss of my memories
of the village...
memories of the Ville.

Buddy's Gone Home

His name was Edward, but that was just legal.
Buddy, it fit him, like the eyes of an eagle.
Our friend was full of peace and grace.
This village was his favorite place.

The changes to the neighborhood,
don't always offer something good.
The Mystic waters are no longer muddy,
and yes, we've lost our good friend Buddy.

I talked with him most every day,
so many stories I've heard him say.
I should have taken better notes.
I can't remember all his quotes.

I do know that he loved the Ville.
It loved him back. It always will.
Buddy was like an uncle to me.
I let him go, reluctantly.

From the time he spent in the military,
to his post office chores down in old Roxbury...
Buddy made serving folk necessary,
in a way that was simply extraordinary.

He helped to transport that Quonset hut,
that served the 'hood 'til the doors were shut.
From the barracks in Charlestown, emerged a home,
in the moving truck of Cleedie Rhone.

He also built his very own house,
and raised three boys with a loving spouse.
That little red cottage still stands today.
Most older homes have faded away.

On Arlington Street, one of those first three,
where Blacks in Medford were allowed to be,
he helped establish community...
and made the outside, look and see.

He challenged Medford to think a bit,
and recognize we also fit,
that here were good and honest people,
that heard the bells and saw the steeple.

He came to us with a Cambridge heart,
but that's not what truly set him apart.
He became a first, an historic affair...
as the Black postmaster in Medford Square.

He put our Village on the map,
Put your hands together, and clap.
Buddy's bag was full of tricks...
He was from 0-2-1-5-6.

He'd weigh that package on the scale,
and always remember to deliver the mail.
Like the pony express on the dusty trail,
he answered the call to serve, without fail.

Even that blizzard in '78,
couldn't make Uncle Buddy late.
They say the strong men keep on coming.
Mr. Clayton kept things humming.

His life could be a graduate study,
though he preferred to just be Buddy.
His photos sit on the Center's walls,
confirming his place in hallowed halls.

Everyone loved him, of this I'm sure.
His motives were always clean and pure.
He'd give the shirt, right off his back,
to red or white or brown or black.

He and my dad were the best of friends,
fishing the Mystic, where the river bends.
Some days they couldn't catch a cold.
But all those memories shine like gold.

They worshipped God and fixed his church,
with plaster and paint and pine and birch.
They'd sip some Saturday evening tea...
Southern Comfort or Wild Tur-key.

They'd play bid whist and never fight,
if other crews --showed up-- trump tight.
Soon that bond will reignite,
and they'll just laugh all through the night.

He outlived most of his closest friends.
He'll see them all, as this chapter ends.
Whit and Frankie and Varnie and Nate,
will all be waiting at Saint Mike's gate.

To Tip, and Dave, and Peter too...
your pops was special, through and through.
And now he joins Sweet Caroline,
a leaf on God's eternal vine.

I've written poems about many things.
I have to say that this one stings.
In him, I see why freedom rings...
and now he soars on angel's wings.

He rose whenever the clock would beep,
and trudged through snows, New England deep.
For he indeed had vows to keep,
and miles to go, before he'd sleep.

Uncle Buddy had vows to keep.
He's done his work...we'll let him sleep.

Dedicated to a West Medford icon,
The irreplaceable Edward L. "Buddy" Clayton
November 11, 1928 - November 14, 2022

Community Servings

The mini food pantries and little libraries adorn our streets,
like "pop-up" vending stalls and brightly festooned food trucks.
We pass them on our COVID-19 constitutionals...
by the fire station, the community center, and the church.

Pastors tell us that there is no ministry,
until a need is met.
Public poverty is a corporate debt,
that must be paid...
out of the tithes of our public trust.
Please send this aid.

The truckers and Lyft drivers prevail.
They get bound folk out of virus jail.
To Walmart they go, over hill and dale,
while white postal trucks deliver the mail.

We owe it to all to see
that we bring each vessel alee,
repairing their leaking hulls,
beneath the circling gulls.

Each boat in the harbor's dock
represents our shared humanity,
represents communal frailty,
our one human family...
one single family tree.

I can't know it all, so I will ask this...
How many deaths are acceptable risk?
Will racial disparities always exist?
Will more Blacks die as the fever persists?
Who decides who the plague should miss?

Why does the knife have to always twist?
Satan too, seems to have a list...
Who can avoid the Judas kiss?

How could so many suffer and die,
while diffident leaders just stand by,
while prideful men give cold alibi,
to the ill-timed sting of the viral lie,
and the scam they seem hell-bound to try?

Meanwhile just people, continue to aid...
as some loved one, to rest is laid.
Seeking to light up the darkening shade,
into the waters of death, they wade.

The word of faith they understood.
They will uphold the public good.
They stoke the fires and gather wood.
They seek to lead, as shepherds should.

They won't spend time on platitudes.
They won't lose ground to attitudes.
They share new grace and gratitude,
and offer the struggling more latitude.

I can't know it all, but I can know this...
The people who love are the ones in bliss.
They're people who yet want to hug and to kiss...
the ones that the solitude makes us miss...
the ones isolation beats like a fist...
the ones that the Father has on His list...
community-builders who yet persist
to wear their hearts on a naked wrist.

Community builders, let's echo this,
and wear our hearts on a naked wrist.

CCSR...We've Got Next

Perhaps you've never heard of us.
That's cool, no need to make a fuss.
C and C and S and R...
This poem will state just who we are.

We are Medford's youthful hope,
many strands of a braided rope,
not seeking notoriety,
as we build a better society.

We're project-driven to get things done,
to make new friends and have some fun.
We look to build community,
by serving with strength and unity.

We gather food, and books and toys
to enrich the lives of girls and boys,
to help our city's hungry and poor,
the ones that fortune may ignore.

We lift each other as we climb,
together achieving a greater design.
Black and white and brown and tan,
we tell each other, yes we can.

We can make the future brighter.
We can make our bonds grow tighter.
We can make the darkness lighter,
showing our mettle as a fighter.

Medford is truly a special place,
but sometimes struggles with class and race.
We meet to talk about this plight,
and strategize to make things right.

In dynamic conversations,
we honor the roots of many nations.
We build new bridges to understand,
the favor that our founder's planned.

If you think this job's for you,
come and join our youthful crew.
Many hands make lighter work,
and having fun's a daily perk.

As we move into the street,
we celebrate each soul we meet.
We search to find our common ground,
and cherish friendships that we've found.

We'll plant a garden to make things grow.
We'll pick up trash the careless throw.
All over Medford we will go,
to move beyond the status quo.

C and C and S and R...
this is our guide, our own North Star,
each word a vital compass point,
to show the values we anoint.

Center---our realm of cooperation.
Citizens---drive a balanced nation.
Sociably sharing opinions and views...
Responsible for the me's and the you's.

Notice there is no "I" in our name.
We don't aspire to singular fame.
We look to serve the common good
by street, and block, and neighborhood.

We've got next...What does that mean?
We're taking the court with a special team.

From schools throughout this Mystic town,
we're black and white and tan and brown.

A civil discourse blesses the people,
even without a shrine or steeple.
Our mission is to spread the love,
envisioned by powers high above.

We are Medford's youthful hope,
learning to create and cope,
within the city where we live...
to have an open heart and give.

C and C and S and R...
this is how we raise the bar...
for city, state and even the nation,
a standard for our generation.

Dedicated to Medford Public School's
Center for Citizenship and Social Responsibility (CCSR)
Richard Trotta, Director
February, 2022

The Twenty-Four Gates to Medford

At the first gate to Medford
the city gave to me,
a school named for my ancestry...

At the second gate to Medford
the city gave to me,
library doors,
and a school named for my ancestry.

At the third gate to Medford
the city gave to me,
Condon Shell shores,
library doors,
and a school named for my ancestry.

At the fourth gate to Medford
the city gave to me
a Poet Laureate,
Condon shell shores,
library doors,
and a school named for my ancestry.

At the fifth gate to Medford
the city gave to me
fried onion rings...
a Poet Laureate,
Condon shell shores,
library doors,
And a school named for my ancestry

At the sixth gate to Medford
the city gave to me
fat geese a-pooping
fried onion rings...

a Poet Laureate,
Condon shell shores,
library doors,
and a school named for my ancestry,

At the seventh gate to Medford
the city gave to me
local beer a-brewing,
Fat geese a-pooping,
fried onion rings...
a Poet Laureate,
Condon shell shores,
library doors,
and a school named for my ancestry.

At the eighth gate to Medford
The city gave to me
J.B's ice cream scoopin',
local beer a-brewing,
Fat geese a-pooping,
fried onion rings...
a Poet Laureate,
Condon shell shores,
library doors,
and a school named for my ancestry.

At the ninth gate to Medford
the city gave to me
Juneteenth flag-raising,
J.B's ice cream scoopin',
local beer a-brewing,
fat geese a-pooping,
fried onion rings...
a Poet Laureate,
Condon shell shores,
library doors,
and a school named for my ancestry.

At the tenth gate to Medford
the city gave to me
coronavirus masking,
Juneteenth flag-raising,
J.B's ice cream scoopin',
local beer a-brewing,
fat geese a-pooping
fried onion rings...
a Poet Laureate,
Condon shell shores,
library doors,
and a school named for my ancestry.

At the eleventh gate to Medford
the city gave to me
park renovations,
coronavirus masking,
Juneteenth flag-raising,
J.B's ice cream scoopin',
local beer a-brewing,
fat geese a-pooping,
fried onion rings...
a Poet Laureate,
Condon shell shores,
library doors,
and a school named for my ancestry.

At the twelfth gate to Medford
The city gave to me
a blue police station,
park renovations,
coronavirus masking,
Juneteenth flag raising,
J.B's ice cream scoopin',
local beer a-brewing,
fat geese a-pooping,

fried onion rings...
a Poet Laureate,
Condon shell shores,
library doors...

and a school named for my ancestry.

(Adapted from the Twelve Days of Christmas, traditional folk carol, ca. 1780)

Gwendolyn's Rhyme

She strolls all over the neighborhood,
like many can't, and others should.
She moves like women half her age,
and won't stay in seniority's cage.

She's got a mischievous twinkling eye...
might tell the truth, might tell a lie.
Doesn't cook or do the dishes,
keeps the women all in stitches.

Drove her car all over the place,
kept a very speedy pace.
Now she's got a young chauffeur,
can't really let her drive no more.

She's from the islands you should know.
That Bajan rhythm has a flow.
It sometimes mesmerizes folk,
especially when she tells a joke.

Man, this lady is filled with spice,
some might say more naughty than nice.
Younger brothers should beware,
her sharp eyes see you over there.

Her bark may sometimes have some bite.
She'll let you know when things aren't right.
She may be just a bit petite,
but she's as tough as the Naval fleet.

Her daughter and her sons made lives,
that go on hold when she arrives.
She's still the boss; she's still the queen.
All her leaves are fresh and green.

If anyone is keeping score,
nine decades done plus ten years more.
Lots of stories she can share.
You don't listen; she don't care!

She's seen the village change its stripes,
but doesn't waste much time on gripes.
Checks in like a good mom should,
knows about the neighborhood.

West Medford's lost so many souls,
who filled so many vital roles.
But God is wise and never fails,
So yes, this elder still prevails.

She's far away from ordinary,
always laughing loud and merry.
She's lived this way a century.
She's the legend; she's Gwen Lee.

Dedicated to West Medford's inimitable Gwendolyn Lee, on the occasion of her 100th birthday, July 10 1922.

Mr. Greene, I Presume

In every life there is a light...
that burns like fire, hot and bright.
illuminating heart and skill,
revealing wisdom...in God's will.

Oscar Greene walked such a road,
carrying the Master's load.
He saw the vision and wrote it down,
with patience, wit, and hardly a frown.

From small epistles of godly advice,
to several books of salt and spice...
his writing was always clean and clear,
elevating the atmosphere.

His *Guidepost* missives edified,
with simple prose that amplified.
Never at a loss for words,
he shepherded the Master's herds.

A kid like me, who yearned to write,
would read and marvel every night.
His words impressed as sure and true,
writing the way, I hoped to do.

A century of trials revealed
much of what the fates concealed.
He told these stories with ageless grace,
seeking his heavenly Father's face.

Oh the places he would go,
new revelations sent to sow...
His perfect grammar and easy flow,
made the pages fairly glow.

They say John Henry was a heck of a man,
leaving this life with hammer in hand.
But Oscar Greene was a prince among men,
his choice of weapons, a keyboard and pen.

Hot and bright his fire burned.
Local fame was surely earned.
All the lessons graciously learned...
all the right corners purposely turned.

A soldier, a husband, a father, and more,
his dearest Ruby has waited a score.
Her beloved now enters eternity's door,
for the milk and honey the angels pour.

This neighborhood will ever cherish
a spirit that will never perish...
a treasured sage for all the city,
generous, wise, urbane, and witty.

Let us remember God's herald well.
He always answered his Father's bell.
And now sweet Ruby hugs her love,
and pearly gates open high above.

Lord receive your faithful son.
His earthly work has long been done.
Seldom has his like been seen.
We'll always remember Oscar H. Greene.

*Dedicated to West Medford's remarkable Oscar H. Green, Sr... Godly scribe and griot...
Rest in gentle peace. May 28, 1918 - June 16, 2022*

Picket Fences

The modern-day home makeover moguls
and real estate robber barons keep coming.
They plaster **"We buy ugly houses"** signs
to telephone poles and fence posts.
The contractor trucks and dumpsters
sit ready beside the porta-potties
and pallets of brick, boards, and broken promises.

Dig-safe has marked out the gas and power lines.
The city has issued all the permits.
The banks approved the financing,
and the harried homeowner has headed south.
North Carolina, Georgia, maybe Tennessee...
somewhere warmer, where their new money
would grant them acreage, three full bathrooms, lots of bedrooms
and a serious man cave.

That old house on Jerome, or Lincoln, or Arlington
was 'sposed to be the inheritance,
built by their daddy's daddy...
or just beyond the red lines,
and purchased for that ten thousand
GI Bill bucks that seemed like a million,
back then...
back when the wink and the nod
between the money-lenders
and the city fathers,
defined the boundaries of a
white man's privilege
and a Black man's prohibition.

Now the heritage is fading.
What used to be that

remarkable Black neighborhood
with the legacy of legends,
war heroes, doctors, shop owners, athletes and artists...
is losing its bronze-hued luster...
losing its proud patina,
to the new shine of subway tiled bathroom spas,
barn wood beams, butler's pantries,
and his and hers Beamers.

The new residents don't
care much about the history...
Old Henry's Little Store and
Faucenia's Beauty Salon and such.
But they do love the basketball courts,
and they laud the city's haste to redo
the tennis courts and such.
They like the green grass and backyard barbecues,
and the walking trails along the river too.
The like the Bloody Mary mornings,
the merlot meet-ups,
and the margarita midnights.

They feel instantly entitled,
and they let the old folks know it.
Meanwhile, the developers keep calling those elders
and their grown-up kin.

We buy ugly houses.
We pay cash, any condition...
Half a mil' sounds like a lot, when you had a devil of a time getting a
ten thousand dollar mortgage
for your little piece of the American dream.

Still, you hang on.
You really love this old place.

You remember when a Black man was the postmaster,
and when the first Negro woman
was elected to the school committee.
You remember how great Charlie Booker was at hockey,
and how good Rudy Smith looked in the PDs dress blues.

You remember letting the little kids
get on those yellow school buses,
to leave the comforts of the Hervey
and go integrate the Wait, the Gleason,
and the Dame.

You remember when the neighborhood
was a tight-knit community
of Doc Kountze datelines,
and O.G's Shiloh sermons,
and Humpty's homeboy haircuts,
and Varnie Carter's sand-finished ceilings.

You fix your face,
'cause you know God don't like ugly.
You wave and you smile politely.
Sometimes they wave or smile back.
Sometime, they don't.

Whatever...

All the while, you're reminiscing 'bout back in the day...
Maybe you're hearing Alan Dawson playing with Dave Brubeck on
that old stereo console...
or Conrad and Levi singing "Peace Be Still" on the corner of
Holton and Bower...
or the doo-woppers on J-Street and Harvard Ave...
reminiscing 'bout the neighborhood,
back in the day,
when the Ville had a soundtrack all its own.

Truth is...
You never actually had a white picket fence...
not quite the statement you were trying to make,
way back then.
You wanted respect, more than assimilation.
You wanted community, more than acceptance.
You wanted the familiar, the faithful,
and the first love.

All the while you wish that the kids would've stayed
and tried to make a go of it here.
But the developers kept calling.
So did Atlanta,
and Raleigh-Durham...
and their own American dreams.

I guess home is where the heart is, but...

You're already tired of condo culture
and bedroom convenience,
of professional dog-walkers,
commuter rail parking spot bandits,
snooty au pairs, and 9-1-1 dialing Karens.
How could the dregs of the city,
given up so grudgingly,
ceded so strategically,
now be the jewel in the Mystic kingdom's crown.

The modern-day home makeover moguls
and real estate robber barons keep coming.
"We buy ugly houses" signs
plastered to telephone poles and fence posts.

Newsflash...

Ain't too many ugly houses left.

Nope, ain't too many left.
Could be a "doo-woppers" refrain,
from that J-Street corner, back in the day...
Shout it out, my brothers.

Ain't too many ugly houses left.
Nope, ain't too many left.

--Allies--

"It is no longer good enough to cry peace. We must seek peace, act peace, and live in peace."

Shenandoah Proverb

Paradox

Somehow, it doesn't matter what we do.
You'll never give us what we're due.
When we play the game better,
you'll attach a scarlet letter.
When we model the best behavior,
you'll anoint a different savior.
When we suggest what's good and true,
you'll say that's good for me, but not for you.
When we defy your algorithm,
you'll create another schism.
If we try to level the playing field,
you'll show up with a sword and shield.
You won't address inequity.
You'd rather steal our dignity.
If we pass your toughest test,
you'll still refuse to call us blessed.
If we advocate for us,
you'll want to kick us off the bus.
If we show anguish and pain,
it seldom penetrates your brain.
No matter what we say or do,
you think this world is just for you.

Friend of Mine

So, we're clearly very different.
I mean beyond the obvious.
You know...the ebony/ivory thing.
There's the age thing.
There's the education thing.
There's the background thing.
There's the experience thing.
There's the frame of reference thing...
and there's the how did you two
ever get connected...thing.

He's seen some things I haven't got a clue about.
I've shown him some things that he wasn't hip to either.
It's been a fair trade.
A good bargain has been made.
No more dues need be paid.
No dragons had to be slayed.
We can call each other friends.

Awkward moments may sometimes arise,
but never enough to darken the skies
and bring real storms
to the seasons of relationship
and the shores of human kindness.

He's a good dude.
There's a patience to the way he goes about his day.
There's a generosity of spirit that guides his resolve
to do the right thing by the folks he deals with.
He's got a little quirky in him,
but he's easy to like.

Then there's the music thing.
The dance his fingers do

over those ivory keys,
and those ebony keys,
at an upright, or a baby grand.
There's the composing,
and the arranging,
and the scoring,
and the conducting,
and the writing...
and the band plays on.

I think he brings out the nerd in me.
I think I amplify his cool.
Poetry and music were made for this...
Technical,
and what the heck-nical.
If you been there,
then you know...
if not,
you might want to ask around,
or listen to some Gil-Scott
and some Thelonious Monk...
straight, with no chaser.

I'm done now...
don't want things to get weird.
You know...
there's the ebony/ivory thing.
There's the age thing.
There's the education thing.
There's the background thing.
There's the experience thing.
There's the frame of reference thing...
and there's the how did you two
ever get connected...thing?

Yessiree,
that's a darn good question.

The Ally

Friends become distant and strange...
as if you have some creeping mange.
Family wonders why and wring their hands.
How could you choose them over us?
We're your blood...
bone of your bone and flesh of your flesh.
They not like us.
They're so different...
less than, not equal to, beneath.
Declarations have been made.
Arrangements are in place.
These are matters of our legacy.
Signs have been painted.
You're going to be cast out.
You're going to be shunned.
You need to stick with your own kind.

An ally...
is that what they're calling you?
Well it's a hard row to hoe.
You're making strange bedfellows.
You're casting your white pearls before swine.
You weren't raised to behave like this.
Our family is a proud and honored clan.
We'll never be lower than any black man.
There's no room for them at this table.
There's always been two sides of the track...
a right and a wrong side of town...
our kind and their kind...
your people, and those folk.
It's gonna' kill your mother,
and your daddy's turning over
in his grave.

You want to shout out
Black lives matter.
But the master plan
is to make them scatter...
to serve them pain
on a silver platter.
Our people owned them.
They worked this land
for two hundred years.
They were our property,
our negroes,
dammit, our niggers,
to make it plain.

You can't be out there with them.
You can't be shoulder to shoulder
with the ones we need to dominate...
relegate...
subjugate...
eliminate.

They want reparations.
Well, we're making preparations,
to give them 40 acres of hell
and a mule kick to the gut.
You don't seem to get it son.
This is the way the race is run.
There's not enough room for everyone.
The time for black and brown is done.
Show your pride and pick up your gun.
Pick the side that has always won.

You can't be out there with them.
You can't be shoulder to shoulder
with the ones we need to dominate...
relegate...
subjugate...
eliminate.

Broken Mirrors

Poet said look at the man in the mirror.
Poet said you ought to change your ways.
Poet said it couldn't be any clearer.
Poet said these are the final days.

Choir sang see your reflection.
Choir sang lift up your gates.
Choir sang stop the rejection.
Choir sang redemption waits.

Prophet taught look deep within this well.
Prophet taught answer this clanging bell.
Prophet taught all the truth he could tell.
Prophet taught justice denied is hell.

Poet said look at the man in the mirror.
Poet said you ought to change your ways.
Poet said it couldn't be any clearer.
Poet said these are the final days.

Justice

The streets call out no justice, no peace.
When will the war against Black folks cease?
When will you say a farewell to arms,
and finally yield to equality's charms?
When will the wounds that run blood red,
no longer mean that a brown boy is dead?

The state of the nation is vile and rank.
Retching with bile, who do we thank?
Political discourse fails to achieve
any good hope that our hearts can conceive.
Block by block there's fire and smoke—
Society smolders. It's chaos; it's broke.

Piles of dreams just rot and congeal,
a sting the children will always feel.
This kind of justice is hardly blind.
It makes no mention of good, or kind.
We know too well why you strangle our vote.
We'd tear down the fences and fill in the moat.

Freedom delayed is just-us denied.
We watch the hollow point bullets glide.
It ain't no magic carpet ride...
no handsome groom and pretty bride.
Toward the abyss we quickly slide,
amid the mounting genocide,
amid the stain of racial pride,
our precious liberties shoved aside...
scorn at every tear that's cried.
You call us brother, and sister...you lied!

Critical theories of racial hate,
you won't let them penetrate
the fundamental institution,
without swift blows of retribution.
You bought the founder's constitution,
without the price of restitution.
You won't let children hear the truth,
for fear that they become like Ruth...
for fear that they will face their kings,
and gain the freedom courage brings.

The streets now edge toward riot and rage.
You'd loose the hatred from every cage,
and soon erase from every page,
any white fault for slavery's wage.
You'd hide the truth from God's own gauge...
But He sees every play you stage.

You will not swallow any pill
that codifies supremacist will.
Instead you seek to normalize,
a sovereign right to sanitize.
You hold no rights self-evident,
except your rights to own, not rent,
except your rights to every cent,
except your rights to close the tent,
except your choice to not repent.

The streets call out, no justice, no peace.
We pray for redemption. We crave release.
We hope against hope for every child,
that urban streets become less wild,
and the gaping wounds that run blood red,
don't again mean that a brown boy is dead.

Inspired by John Dalton and Spheres of Influences' jazz composition "Justice", March 2022

Bystander's Lullaby

Is it well my brother,
to just stand idly by...
and watch them kill a black man,
to watch him slowly die?

They kill one for the master.
They kill one for the dame.
They kill the innocent little boy,
who lives down the lane.

Is it well my white friend,
to turn and walk away,
while men of foul intention
rule each waking day?

Laws to keep fair treatment blocked,
laws to keep the prisons stocked,
and one law written specially...
to keep the borders locked.

Is it well fair maidens,
to quiet now your voice,
and follow in blind silence...
the clearly evil choice?

Silence for the victim,
silence for his kin,
silence for the race of those,
who wear his darker skin.

Is it well within your soul,
to hang your head in shame...
and never offer stern rebuke
for the cruel and sinful game?

Rebuke for the hatred...
rebuke for the pride,
and even for the privilege,
of watching from the side.

Is it well Dame Justice,
to just stand idly by...
as the dreams of countless brown kids fail,
without a reason why?

No dreams on the corner.
No dreams on the street.
No dreams for the innocent lass,
covered by the sheet.

The Fog of War

We can't even measure our lives
by the decades...
by the years...
by the months...
by the weeks...
by the days...
by the hours...
and by the minutes.

We now have to measure our lives
by the haters...
by the trials...
by the bigots...
by the racists...
by the instigators...
by the victims...
and by the killers.

America's heading for such a train wreck.
When did these cards come into the deck?
People are shouting, "Yo, what the heck?"
Why does the knee have to crush the neck?
Who do peace officers serve and protect?
Why is there such abuse and neglect?
Who closed the door to the word respect?
What kind of change can our protests effect?
What righteous God would refuse to object?
What kind of world can our children expect?

Have we yet again become the poet's
prophetic hogs...
penned up ingloriously,
hemmed up laboriously,

hunted down injuriously,
shouted down most furiously,
delayed most notoriously,
denied most victoriously?

These are the decades of new death.
These are the years of new yokes.
These are the months of new menace.
These are the weeks of new worry.
These are the days of new demons.
These are the hours of new horror.
These are the moments of new mayhem.

How can a nation be so off-course...
all of our progress now in reverse...
MLK's dream in a funeral hearse.
Don't call a doctor; don't need a nurse.
The aim is to kill, and they always shoot first.
The signs all point to it getting worse,
more evil eyes than a voodoo curse.
Not enough coin in the federal purse,
but the corporate coffers they will reimburse.

You've beckoned your poor and disenfranchised,
to hate, agitate, and castigate our poor and disenfranchised...
when they really should be one with us, through the fog
of your war on the poor.
You've bewitched your middle class with envy, scorn and disgust
about our middle class, and their so-called entitlements...
When in reality your women, and your children, and your families
have benefitted far more from government subsidy.
You've cheated charity and broken philanthropy in more ways
than there are days.
Meanwhile you've turned vast sums of American wealth
and tax-time dodges
toward campaigns of marginalization, suppression, and exclusion.

We can't even afford to imagine
plowshares and picket fences.
We can't even try to envision
growing old and comfortable together.
We can't even begin to talk legacy and heritage
with our children, and our children's children.
You've so completely enveloped us
in the smoke of urban flames...
and the fog of war.

There you stand, race proud and irritated...
ready to shoot at the melanated.
Cul-de-sacs are closed and gated...
targets acquired and traps fully baited...
military ordinance incorporated...
young black lives expiration dated.
How are these lives so worthlessly rated?
To the killing fields we're now relegated.
Why is our future so painfully-fated?

Martin's not coming back through the door.
We don't have that kind of King anymore.
Who lowers this ceiling and raises this floor?
Who pulls down these walls, and empowers the poor?
How many times must we must protest and prove...
assemble, invoke, and begin then to move?
We find ourselves back in that late sixties groove.
Is this a path that can ever be smooth?

We can't even measure our lives
by the decades...
by the years...
by the months...
by the weeks...
by the days...
by the hours...
or by the minutes.

We now have to measure our lives
by the militias and the minions...
by the instigators and the insurrectionists...
by the bump stocks and black talons...
by the ones in fatigues and flak jackets...
by the ones in riot gear and advancing blue lines...
by the ones in wrapped in confederate flags...
by the ones in business suits and golf pants...
by the ones on Twitter and the dark web.

Through the fog of war,
we see a different America—
a scabrous blight on the amber waves...
the purple mountains reduced to rubble...
the lady in the harbor cuffed and muzzled...
the beacon in the bay gone dark and silent...
red blood flowing in the streets...
blue lines bracing for the looters and cheats...
white cloth cut into peaked hoods and sheets.

You've enslaved our people for doleful decades.
You've endangered our people for Yankee years.
You've entangled our people for monstrous months.
You've ensnared our people for woeful weeks.
You've encroached on our people for disastrous days.
You've envied our people for hateful hours.
You've endured our people for measured minutes.

You would again consign us to the ash heap of history.
You would again declare us 3/5ths of a man.
You would again make us those hunted hogs.
You would again confine us to cabin and field.
You would forever fly your banners of disdain over us.
You would forever deny our achievements and contributions.
You would forever incarcerate and disappear us.
You would forever avow that our lives don't matter.

These are the decades of new death.
These are the years of new yokes.
These are the months of new menace.
These are the weeks of new worry.
These are the days of new demons.
These are the hours of new horror.
These are the moments of new mayhem.

Still, even through the fog of war,
we see a different America—
a marvelous light at the tunnel's end...
the purple mountains redolent with hope and mercy...
the lady in the harbor released and renewed...
the beacon in the bay beckoning the lost, the stolen,
and the strayed...
red blood flowing through a unified heart...
blue lines embracing a true call to serve and protect...
white cloth sewn into choir robes and garments of praise.

We are not afraid.
We will not be cowed.
We will not be silent.
We will know our friends
and stay beside them.
God is on our side.
Justice will roll down like waters...
righteousness like an ever-flowing stream.
If we must die...
it will not be as hogs to the slaughter.
We too are Americans.
We will not let hate win.
We
shall
overcome.

Ballots, Not Bullets

I need for you to ache about the plight of the first people of this land,
who shared this land, then lost this land to the usurper, the invader, the
liar, the killer, the lawmaker, and the conqueror.

I need for you to see the bowels of a 17th century British bark packed like
a sardine can with the diseased and desecrated bodies of African chattel.

I need for you to imagine the violated carcasses of my beautiful Black
sisters and brothers thrown into the ocean,
passing turbulently from this life to the next.

I need for you to see that the founders and the framers
were just men.
They were flawed. They weren't gods or saints, and they weren't in any
way prepared for this.

I need for you to imagine the sting of the cat-o-nine tails,
the burning lye, the manacles, the stocks, the chains
and thick ropes, on raw brown flesh.

I need for you to understand who built a cotton and corn
and tobacco and sugar cane economy,
fueled an industrial revolution,
made the first families of a new nation millions upon millions
of old American dollars, and have still not been made whole
for the myriad sins against them.

I need for you to see all of this...to feel all of this...
to be affected and moved by all of this.

I need for you to see that the Massachusetts 54th,
and the Buffalo Soldiers, and the Tuskegee Airmen,
and the Harlem Hellfighters were American heroes too.

Heroes that fought for the liberty of a nation, the safety of a world,
and the dignity of a race...a race that is still denied all
of that dignity and many attendant equal protections under the law.

This franchise that we honor and are fighting for yet again
is sacrosanct and sacrificial and so fragile. Bullets flew
and still fly at us, as we mark out those hard-won ballots.

I need for you to remember that time when we were defined as 3/5ths
of a man, less than and never equal to...to realize that Juneteenth did
not deter Jim Crow,
did not dissuade the night riders,
and that the Klan burned crosses and tied nooses and perfected home
grown terrorism to prevent this.

I need for you to know that Malcolm and Medgar and Martin
marched, bled, and died for this...
to recognize that Josephine Baker, and Richard Wright,
and James Baldwin, and Claude McKay quit being Americans
to cry out for this...

I need for you to know that teenagers got on buses and traveled to the
deepest, darkest hearts of Dixie to pursue this... that brave Black folk
and committed allies defied the dogs, and the hoses, the fire-bombings,
and those white robes and pointed hoods to pursue this.

I need for you to see the charred bodies of lynching victims
in old black and white photos.
I need for you to feel the historical anguish of Emmett Till's family.
I need for you to feel the horrific anguish of Schwerner, Goodman and
Chaney's families.

I need for you to know the true courage of Joseph Cinque, Denmark
Vesey, Nat Turner, Harriet and Sojourner, Ruby Bridges,
James Farmer, Mary McCloud Bethune, Diane Nash, and John Lewis.

I need for you to know that histories which detail the truth of this are
being threatened with erasure and elimination...
that histories which intentionally disappear the mention of this
are being newly written and rushed to press.

I need for you to see the emerging front of new civil strife
being birthed in the heartland and the hinterland, in the courts,
the churches, the country clubs, and the capitol buildings.

I need for you to know that the radical right is shouting
in full throat and plain sight to be rid of everything
that makes us whole for the myriad of sins against us.

This franchise that we honor and are fighting for yet again
is sacrosanct and sacrificial and so fragile. Bullets flew
and still fly at us, as we trudge toward the bridges we must cross, and the
polling places we must secure.

So many bullets...

I need for you to understand that bad cops
perpetrate daily atrocities and fail to protect,
in spite of this franchise.
That good cops cross the thin blue line of silence
to offer real protection for this franchise.

I need for you to feel the anguish of Amadou Diallo's family.
I need for you to feel the anguish of Breonna Taylor,
and George Floyd, and Ahmaud Arberry's families.

I need for you to see that the founders and the framers
were just men. They were flawed. They weren't gods or saints,
and they weren't in any way prepared for this.

I need for you to look at the senate and the house
and the supreme court and know that power concedes nothing,
without a demand.
They mean to have their way with us again... to codify, constrain, and
confine us to less than, to not equal, to an inconvenient truth that
cannot replace the rightness of their whiteness.

I need for you see the gaudy color photos of a Texas family
awash in a sea of rifles, pistols, semi-automatic
and super high-powered military style ordinance... smiling
at a corrupted constitutional interpretation.

So many bullets...

I need for you agonize with women who now have to surrender the
right to choose what happens to their bodies in pregnancy...
to agonize over the return of back alley abortions
and a thousand assaults on their reproductive rights.

I need for you to feel the consistently unnatural heat
of a warming planet, and fear the rising tide of the earth's oceans,
and face down the deniers and destroyers and debauchers
of field, forest, and stream.

I need for you to see the masked faces of the Proud Boys and the
Patriot Front and a thousand other hate groups as they openly parade
on American thoroughfares and fix their gaze
and their guns on new final solutions.

So many bullets...

I need for you to sympathize with mothers from Sandy Hook
and Uvalde, and fathers from Highland Park and Tulsa,
and brothers and sisters from Columbia, and Blacksburg,

and Miami, and Las Vegas, and Buffalo.

I need for you to see that the founders and the framers
were just men. They were flawed. They weren't gods or saints,
and they weren't in any way prepared for this.

I need for you to see all of this...to feel all of this...to be affected and
moved by all of this.

Perhaps then, all of us will take these thousand feelings
and convert them into urges, impulses, and footsteps.
Those of us that can run, will run.
Those of us that can walk, will walk.
Those of us that can crawl or be carried, will be lifted and led.
Those of us that now know that we must be the change,
those of is that know that all politics begin in the heart,
extend to the home...
and penetrate the hood,
will take it to the streets, yet again.

Those of us that have learned that justice delayed
is justice denied, will carry the fight to the polling places, and the
mailboxes, and the ballot drops.

We will convince ourselves that silence is a luxury we can't afford.
We will convict ourselves in duty we can't avoid.
We will comfort ourselves in the embrace of kindred spirits.
We will hasten to cling to the best we've seen in each of us,
and want to be in that number...
We will be sworn allies with those
that have measured us by the content of our character,
and not the color of our skin,
or the nap of our hair,
or the way we choose to love,

and whom we choose to make a life with...
or why our tent must be bigger.

Here is the essence of what I came to note.
This is the bay for a brand new boat.
Hope is audacious and can help us to float.
But to cross this deadly river,
we must get out and vote.

This is the way we traverse the castle's moat,
each a living stripe of Joseph's vibrant coat.
This is the prophecy the poet-herald wrote...
to cross this ugly ocean,
we must get out and vote.

Victories of the past, we can't afford to gloat.
Herein lies the lesson of all the lines I quote.
To counter all that ails us, we need an antidote.
To cross the gulf that shames us,
we must get out and vote.

A Call to Action

In the big cities
and the small towns alike,
America sees
a dangerous spike.
Violent intent has reemerged,
as purveyors of lies and hate converge,
to weave a dark and
angry story,
and rob the flag
of all its glory.

We're all called warriors
in this fight.
Let us coalesce
to get things right,
and battle for a common goal,
that speaks to our collective soul,
advancing the causes
of truth and peace,
striving to make
the outrage cease.

That is the call of allyship,
an anchor for this human trip,
not a political bargaining chip,
a die-lock chain, to pull and grip.

When the village gathers to raise a barn,
everyone eats good food from the farm.
When the village gathers to raise its young,
no hate speech is on its tongue.

Dr. King called for beloved community,
faith and grace and love and unity...

Can these fragrant oils grant us immunity?
When all around us, folks hate with impunity?

Some would suggest that his time has passed.
They shoulder their rifles ready to blast.
But I submit that this small faction,
will not survive our call to action.
And yes, there will be casualties,
slings and arrows and injuries.
Power yields nothing without a demand.
Racism has to be purged from the land.

We're not a post-racial society.
If you think so, check your sobriety.
The stain of our hubris and piety
is not the most wholesome variety.
Martin preached universal love,
a sacred charge from God above.
There's got to be a real attraction.
This is the quest of our call to action.

I come with his dream in full display,
to spread his truth in a poet's way.
My hope is that you'll hear this verse,
and work to end racism's curse.
Blacks and Jews and Asian kin,
we did not choose our colored skin.
We do not choose to generate,
the ugly power of racial hate.

The time is now to unite our front...
to shoulder the burden and bear the brunt.
For certainly, our foes will seek,
to make our kinship strange and weak.
Let's not allow their prideful rages,
to force us into a thousand cages.

Let's put our smaller wants aside,
and be the voice that's unified.

We can begin right where we are.
We can be those that raise the bar.
We can show a fractured land,
a hopeful future that's now at hand.
Look to make a friend today,
to gather together and yes, to pray.
Regardless of which god you serve,
touch a heart and strike a nerve.

Such was the choice that Martin made...
And for that choice, he dearly paid.
Let's make sure his sacrifice,
steers the ship that breaks the ice.

We're all called warriors
in this fight.
Let us coalesce
to get things right...
and battle for a common goal,
that speaks to our collective soul,
advancing the causes
of truth and peace,
striving to make
the outrage cease.

When this village gathers,
as allies strong,
as beloved cousins,
let's get along.
Across the borders
of neighborhood,
let's be about
the common good.

We're all called warriors
in this fight...
Let's walk in peace,
and truth,
and light.

Maybe

Maybe if we could all cry together,
we could make it all right.
We could wash each other
in familiar tears, bathing away
the dirt of a filthy world,
with something like
a warm spring rain.

Maybe if we could all grieve as one,
over the confusion and mayhem and death
of a society gone more than a bit mad,
we could get past the anger.
We could get out the anxiety.
We could get around the fear.
We could get to real conversation.
We could get on with forgiveness.

Maybe if we could put down our weapons,
we could recover the peaceable kingdom.
We could rekindle lost relationships.
We could embrace human diversity.
We could rediscover beloved community.
We could be equal sons, daughters, and heirs
to a loving and liberating God.

Maybe if we could pick up our crosses
and carry them together, toward the hills of salvation,
we could see each other's footprints
in the sand, and snow, and unpaved byways.
We would know our neighbors.
We would see the road unfold before us.
We would feel the same wind in our sails.
We would value the journey, beyond the destination.

Maybe if we could prize people over possessions,
everyone could have enough to thrive.
Everyone could flourish, not just survive.
Everyone could learn to really give.
Everyone could value the life we live.
Everyone could lift, as we all try to climb.
No one would ever leave his brother behind.

Maybe if we could all laugh together,
we could hear the universal sound of joy.
We could revel in the gurgle of all the babies.
We could immerse ourselves in the sweetness
of each sparkling smile,
the heartiness of each chortle, chuckle,
guffaw and belly laugh.
We could let our frozen guard down,
and warm to the thawing
of a kindred humanity.

Maybe...just maybe.

--Memory--

"*Those we love never truly leave us. They live on in stories, family traditions and legacies that last for generations.*"

Chief Gary Batton, presiding leader of the Oklahoma Choctaw Nation

Serenity

Once a man or woman,
but twice a baby too...
this seems the natural way of things.
It couldn't be more true.

Although you've lived a century...
and weathered every storm,
I change your diaper daily.
That's once again the norm.

Your speech is urgent gibberish,
I've learned to understand.
You cry out and you flail your arms,
in making each demand.

I don't hold this against you,
though my patience may run thin.
This surreal role reversal,
is just the stage we're in.

Your memory has been slipping.
You sometimes cannot tell,
that I'm that blessed infant,
you claimed from heaven fell.

So now this child you treasured
and treated with such care,
manages your every need,
each grey and crinkled hair.

A dozen medications,
they've prescribed for your condition.
Religiously I push them down,
to sponsor your remission.

You curse me like a sailor,
when you're angry or in pain.
Still you are a cherished gift,
I try not to complain.

And to my sons and daughters,
I make this humble plea...
do not shed my wrinkled hide,
when old age gets to me.

Do not think me useless,
and place me in a home,
where underpaid, uncaring hosts
just leave me alone.

Let me move toward heaven,
from a safe, familiar place.
Let me have my dignity
and a measure of God's grace.

Once a man or woman,
for the second time a child,
this rebirth isn't pretty.
The symptoms are not mild.

I've written down the history
for our young ones to remember...
each amazing year you've lived,
every flickering ember.

Every victory you've achieved,
amid life's twists and turns,
every answer you've conceived,
are lessons they have learned.

The little lamb you once led
into pastures full and green,
has now become your shepherd,
toward fields peaceful and serene.

A Life Well-lived

This aging stuff is real,
and it ain't necessarily graceful either...

Stuff be cracking and creaking...
It frankly has me freaking.

Sitting, standing, reaching...
painful lessons it is teaching.

It's not pretty.
I make snorts, cackles, grunts and sighs...
so often, that it mortifies
my thirty year-old sensibilities
of the brother I think I'm s'posed to be.

Oh noble youth...
sagacity and veracity and tenacity
seem so overrated,
when what you long for is
agility and virility
and some distance from senility.

I can remember roller-skating
at the Bal-a-Roue in 1972,
but now I don't know where my glasses are,
when they're sitting right on top of my head.
Why did I even get out of bed?
Oh yeah, I had to go pee.
Shouldn't have had that last cup of tea.
My continence ain't what it used to be.

This aging stuff is real.
Gettin' that check from the government,
Social Security payin' my rent,

won't ever get back all the money I lent.
Don't even matter,
it's already spent.

New diseases at every turn...
case of shingles made my skin burn.
Medical jargon I have to learn,
like merit badges I try to earn.
Wearin' a mask and washin' my hands,
that's what this Covid thing demands...
different shots and different brands.

So many things on my bucket list...
a lot of fine ladies
I never kissed.
A Rolex has never adorned my wrist.
And the mega-millions,
I guess I just missed.

So many friends are
dead and gone.
I cried for them all,
but I had to move on.
Stings quite a bit,
but what can you do,
'cept thank the Lord
that He didn't call you.

I'm growing older every day.
Seniority, that thing just don't play.
So I should cherish the narrow way.
And in God's purpose always stay...
with legacy to pass along,
that keeps my children brave and strong,
that keeps the dial on positive,
and strives to be a life well-lived.

Dixieland Haiku

Road trip headed South.
Got kin in Mississippi.
Catfish and cornbread.

Took Papa's green book...
Had it in the Ford's glove box.
Can't be wrong out here.

Deathly scared of dogs.
These were trained to maul Black flesh.
They'd set them on us.

Birmingham was hot.
Montgomery was hotter.
Selma was pure hell.

We'll kill these black boys
before we'll give them a vote.
This is Dixie son.

Lynch mob came for Bo.
Said he fondled that white girl.
Strung him up right quick.

They burned those girls up.
Set God's house ablaze and laughed.
Was God laughing too?

Bruh Bill had to leave.
White boys say he uppity.
Demopolis, damn.

Them nigras want what?
Forty acres and a mule...
Reparations hell...

Shotgun shacks for blocks...
That's how we livin' down here...
our side of the tracks.

Seven Brown Sisters

Seven brown sisters
sitting on the stoop,
lots of love and friendship
flowing through the group.

One girl is braiding
another's kinky hair,
twisting up each oiled strand
with confidence and care.

Three girls get up
to jump some double-dutch.
The other girls just holler,
enjoying this so much.

Lots of juicy stories
they share with boundless glee,
laughing hard and clapping hands
for all the block to see.

There is no hint of envy.
They all have made a pact,
to look out for each other,
and have each other's back.

When did we lose this gift
within our neighborhood?
The kindness and the fond regard,
is it gone for good?

Now, upon the internet,
bullying and hostility,
memes and vulgar hazing,
replacing all civility.

Racist tropes demean
the places where we live.
Hateful words and images,
refute the love we give.

The times, they are so different,
so filled with worsening gloom.
Parents drag kids off the streets,
fearing the face of doom.

But seven brown sisters
won't restrain their joy.
They're safe within a village,
that no demons can destroy.

Decent folks will call them,
home soon, one by one.
Supper and the street lights
signal night has come.

Seven brown sisters
skip arm-in-arm to school.
Some kids call them uppity.
Some kids call them cool.

They study hard and get good grades,
each and every one.
And still they always seem to find
time for good, clean fun.

When schoolgirl days have passed them by
they graduate with style,
then leave the pomp and circumstance,
to walk a separate mile.

They embrace the H-B-C-Us,
for new matriculations.
Howard, Fisk and Spelman...
all classic destinations.

That's the way they knew it
when each was young at heart,
before their dreams and destinies
drew them all apart.

Before the world of privilege
set in place affairs,
that broke beloved community
and stole those happy stairs.

Before the brownstone raptors
gobbled up their stoops,
replacing all the home girls,
with richer, whiter groups.

So seven sweet brown sisters,
made a facebook page.
They post their pics and progress,
and fight a godless age.

They do a Zoom call monthly,
and pray for one another.
They each lament their daily trials.
and celebrate their mothers.

They plan a girl's retreat
and meet up every year...
no husbands, kids, or politics,
just laughter, wine and cheer.

Master's and some Ph.D's,
each has fine credentials...
Still they relish family, faith...
love, and life's essentials.

There is no hint of envy.
They all have made a pact,
to look out for each other,
and have each other's back.

Memorial Day Reveille

They never returned.
They were the sepia-toned photograph
that sat on the coffee table,
encased in silver and glass.

They became that fateful knock on the door,
or that neatly folded flag
handed to a sniffling widow,
or a grieving mother,
at the end of the last rites.

They were the popular athletes
and the one most likely to succeed,
and the shy, intense kid,
and the brown boys
from the other side of the tracks.

They were uniformed symbols
of an American way of life,
a national esprit de corps,
and a struggle to make the world a better place,
despite homeland struggles with color and caste and race.

They didn't come back.
They became lawns that didn't get mowed,
and homes that fell to disrepair,
and picket fences that never got built.

They became postage stamp commemorations,
and American Legion libations,
and the trials and tribulations
of the ones they left behind.

They are the small oak box of ribbons
and medals, letters from the field,
and faded pictures of the smiles they left behind,
and the way they were.

Doughboys, deck-hands, fly-boys, grunts, GI Joes,
and the few and the proud...
They went where angels feared to tread.
They saw the bullets fly
and watched countless bands of brothers die...
for ideas and ideals and duty and honor.

They witnessed the rocket's red glare
and the bombs bursting in air...
Perhaps they fell silent,
before flags not yet there.

But the flags are here today,
waving in spring's embrace of the epic,
and the heroic, and the unforgotten.
On a thousand grassy fields,
in a thousand cities and towns...
like yours and mine and ours.

Celebrating America's Black Veterans on Memorial Day,
May 29, 2023

Requiem for the Senator

From out of Demopolis, awash in Red clay—
came a Boston icon some poets say.
He sang a little doo-wop back in the day,
with brothers and cousins, crooning hey, hey, heyyy...

Mutton-chop sides and a sculpted 'fro,
this Malcolm-type brother was down for the show.
Loved his mama, sweet Mary Alice—
got into stuff, but without any malice.

Loved his sisters, Shirley and 'Bert—
all of them raised on Demopolis dirt.
With L.J., Joe, Hank, Johnny and Rob...
came up to Boston, for hope and a job.

From the 'Pan, to the Dot', then up to the 'Bury—
stood out among the ordinary.
Liked to debate the affairs of the land,
could go there and take a principled stand.

Became a new voice for the common man,
then a voice in the House with a solid plan.
Became a strong voice for down-trodden masses,
then made Senators get up off their...sssshhhh—

Y'all know where this poet must go.
Can't say the word, so act like you know.
First to call out "the wealthy elite",
a notion Obama would later repeat.

Taking to task the one percent,
who take all the credit and don't pay no rent.
This Senator, like a black light lamp,
would light up the flaws in the white folks camp.

Always a stand on health education—
a singular voice for Black reparations—
adept at creating impact legislation—
always demanding the best from our nation.

Stood tall beside Boston's leading men,
Landsmark, Mel King and Bolling back when—
a Mayor named White, watched Louise Day Hicks
and Southie boys with bats and sticks.

William brought the fight to the street—
no hint of surrender, no hint of retreat.
He fought with his head, his heart and his feet—
victories many, but few real defeats.

Fought to keep Black brothers healthy—
Created wealth, while others got wealthy—
Knew how to do things, big things, you feel me.
Knew how to do things, good things, to heal me.

A green revolution in Abuja—
promoting clean solar in Africa.
Community housing in Roxbury—
Mandela Homes, an LLP.

Created SOMBWA for Black business aid—
Owens made sure some brothers got paid.
The Urban League and the NAACP—
looking for ways to set folks free...
From the New School for Children to Project JESI—
looking for ways to set folks free...

The Founding Director of H.E.L.P.—
looking for ways to set folks free...
Dedicated funding for AIDS/HIV—
looking for ways to set folks free...

Schooling our kids in Black history—
looking for ways to set folks free...
Thirty million bucks to build RCC—
looking for ways to set folks free.

From out of Demopolis, can you believe,
what this country boy would grow to achieve.
On these Boston streets he became quite a fella,
and could still hold a tune, no doubt acapella.

From Beacon Hill to Hazleton Street—
Bill Owens, a man you may want to meet.
On the wings of eagles and swift hind's feet.
Senator, now may your slumber be sweet.

Honoring the late Senator William Owens, Sr.
of Boston, Massachusetts
Redux, February, 2022

A Song for Sidney

The old guard is passing...
screens going black across the nation,
footlights and spotlights turned off.
How do you replace the irreplaceable,
forget the unforgettable,
un-write the indelible?

Ossie, Ruby, Diahann, Dorothy,
Cicely, Brock, Lena, so many...all gone
to that great playhouse in the sky,
or Cabin in the Sky perhaps...

They were first-namers...
soloists, headliners
sirens, soldiers, singers...
Brilliance, greatness, poignancy,
mystery, command, comedy,
courtliness...for God and country.
Actors...advocates...change agents...
the ones that the Great White Way and Tinseltown
so frequently refused to see, to honor,
to emulate, replicate, duplicate...
accommodate.

I remember Sidney Poitier...
the fighter, the lover,
the teacher, the preacher,
the worker, the boss.
How do I requite his loss?
How do I say goodbye to yesterday?
How do I say so long to Mr. Chips and Mr. Tibbs?

Kudos to the Academy for finally doing the right thing.
Kudos to a real President for immediately doing the right thing.
Kudos to the land for lamenting the loss of a good thing.

I remember Sidney...
elegant, fierce,
compassionate, contained,
eloquent, and explosive...
the lily of the field,
and the humble, human soul.

He said it better than a poet ever will...
"If I'm remembered for having done a few good things,
and if my presence here has sparked some good energies,
that's plenty."

I suspect the screens will shine for you again now.
Footlights and spotlights will glow with special radiance.
Though we cannot replace the irreplaceable,
forget the unforgettable,
or un-write the indelible...
Your presence among us has truly
sparked some good energies.
Sleep well...sweet, fair Bahamian prince.
You've done more than "plenty".
And we will somehow make it be enough.

Remembering Sidney Poitier, an American treasure...
February 20, 1927 to January 6, 2022

Ode to Vin Scully

I could've been Vin Scully.
I'm a poet and I know my sports.
People always say,
"you're so articulate."
I like to host things,
to give folks great memories.

Bryant Gumble tried.
Tirico is still at it...gallantly.
But Vin had staying power.
Baseball maven, broadcaster, story-teller...
didn't matter,
Scully could do it all...
emphatically, quietly, or poetically.

That's how I would've done it...
the right call for every moment.
Switching code like nobody's business,
raising the eyebrows of white folk.
How does he do that?

Switching back for the brothers...
but not that Steven A. foolishness,
all bluster and braggadocio,
more like Mike Wilbon and Stuart Scott,
"cool as the other side of the pillow,"
genuine, but clean and understated.

Scully never lost his chops.
He knew how to say it,
no matter who he was saying it to...
the right call for every moment.
Robinson to Guerrero...
Koufax to Fernando.

LA is a great big freeway...
Angelenos grooved on how
he paved the road to grand slams and perfect games.
They try to be so chill about most things.
But game always respects game...
and Vin Scully had big-time game.

Dedicated to the indefatigable Vin Scully, broadcaster and HOF baseball icon, November 29, 1927 to August 2, 2022.

Forever Jimmy Brown

Social justice and civil rights icon, check.
World class lacrosse and NFL football legend, check.
Hero, idol, and inspiration to Black boys and men for decades, check.
Hollywood firebrand and action film stalwart, check.
The strongest, the bravest, the coolest brother around, check!

God must have carved the man out a solid block of onyx stone.
No mold would ever have held his unforgivable,
unapologetic,
un-relenting blackness in (yes), check.

Perfect?
Absolutely not.
He would tell you so himself...many times.

Still,
we are diminished as a race by his passing.
We are diminished as a nation by his passing.
We are diminished as humankind by his passing.

This man, I will truly miss.
May he rest gently in whatever Elysian Fields,
a boundless God chooses for his eternity.

Dedicated to the memory of "The Man" James Nathaniel "Jim" Brown,
February 17, 1936 to May 18, 2023.

Poem for the Playwright, the Pastor, and the Poet

We had no idea where she was taking us.
We heard she had a very vivid imagination,
and liked a little bit of foolishness in her Sweet Tea.
But something in our spirits just said go.
She sounded like she knew what she was doing.
Such boldness and confidence in a Sister
can be very compelling.

She had a preternatural sense of time and place,
and a love for language, rhythm, dialogue, and dialect.
It was like she had been to all the places
she wanted us to go...more than once...
like she had seen it all and taken really good notes.
Those Zora Neale Hurston, Alice Walker, Lorraine Hansberry
kind of notes.
The details of the thing mattered.

I wondered if she was picking on me sometimes...
in that big brother, little sister, kind of way...
in that "look at what I can do" kind of way.
She had me "graveyard dead"
a couple 'a times.
I kind of got used to laying in a coffin.
At this age and stage, I'm not trying to
get into another one anytime soon.

She knows funny as well as she knows God.
And she knows God better than most.
She listens when He talks to her.
She's been through some things,
and she's never cursed Him out for real.
Though I suspect she'll have a question or two

for the Almighty,
when they finally meet up.

I'd done a lot of acting before we met.
I played Oscar Madison, half of "The Odd Couple"
on the Little Theater stage at Fisk University.
She wasn't all that impressed.
She was inclined to say,
It don't take all that...and
respect is earned...one playbill at a time.

Oh, and then there's the poetry thing.
I quickly added her to my short list
of literary lionesses,
Muses to my lyrical spirit...
Maya, Nikki, Sonia, Toni, and Gwendolyn.

We would do tandem pieces
and sling literary longing at one another
on Jubi-Cov couples nights...
Church folk would "ooh and aah"...
But it wasn't no thing.
Poets get after life sometimes...
No, seriously.

G-Dub would lay down some jazzy licks
on that Korg, or Roland, or Yamaha keyboard,
and we'd exchange je ne sais quoi,
and copacetic, and vamos a ponerlo en marcha.
Church folk would "say whaaat",
"and oh no they didn't..."
But it wasn't no thing.
Poets get after life sometimes...
No, seriously.

They invited me and Aunt Che
into the studio when they cut their CD,
Che talkin' 'bout "Me and My Fender Rhodes",
and me recollecting Ahmad Jamal's "Poinciana...
We both knew it was an audience
with a true Queen.
Such boldness and confidence in a Sister
can be very compelling.

When the neighborhood changed,
and some of the fellowship headed Southward,
Lamentations became more than just a chapter
in the good book.
The Living Water receded just a bit.
But that's another poem
for another benediction.

She would say...
"It's like scrambled eggs. Once an egg is all mixed together,
you can't separate it ever again. Too complicated...
You either have to make an omelette or throw them away."
And yes, she always managed
to feed everybody delicious omelettes,
filled with the fruit of the spirit,
and the spice of life.
The Pastor dutifully cares for His flock.
The Pastor rightly divides the Word.
The Pastor loves, really, really hard.

She knows His will as well as she knows her walk.
And she knows her walk better than most.
She sees the path clearly and moves in her gifting.
She's been through some things,
and she's never cursed Him out for real.
Though I suspect she'll have a question or two
for God the Father,
when they meet face to face...

She wasn't from 'round here from the get-go.
So the expectation that she wasn't going to
go back to being a "Southern Belle" somewhere,
at some point...
was probably an unreasonable one...
even for her New England besties.

Temple Worshippers are all over the country these days.
So why not her?
Jubi-cov preachers are all over the country these days.
So why not her?
The "Sound of Jubilee" is all over the world these days,
So why not hers?

Surely she has an idea of where God is taking her.
Although He doesn't always tell us.
Doesn't really have to,
He's got it like that.
Something in her spirit just says go.
It still sounds like she knows what she is doing...
and such boldness and confidence in a Sister
can be very compelling.

Love you Sister-Pastor-Poet-Playwright Robyn Rease...
Fair winds and safe travels, always!
July 25, 2021

Memory Café Moments

Please, please turn on the light.
The darkness really dims my sight.
Living in a foggy daze...
I'm stuck in old age's maze.

So many days I try to keep
the passing moments I feel so deep.
Every time I give a gift,
it gives my heart a great big lift.

What are these suits—
these suits we wear?
Do they reflect
the souls we share?

Pale I was,
so I went for a sail.
After the man untied his bow,
he picked up the oars and started to row.

It was a very bad year,
when they gave the crown to a clown.
When you're picked to rule,
you must have a decent tool.

Come follow my lead.
We'll find what you need.
Let's make space for race...
the human race.

I hope that I can summon the grace,
to accept that I am in the right place.
I wake up each morning with a goal,
determined to achieve it in my soul.

One summer day,
I was flying my kite.
But with so little wind,
it never took flight.

I cannot believe how fast you grow,
almost as fast as a melting snow.
Prose and toes and noses,
so it goes with love and roses.

I once went on a date,
and he became my mate.
Today it's 26 years.
We accept your claps and cheers.

Together we wrote a poem,
with rhyming words and thoughts.
Humans made this happen...
no AI or chat-bots.

From the Memory Café at Jewish Family & Children's Services
with Poet Laureate Terry E. Carter
June 2, 2023

--Mayhem--

"Only two relationships are possible, to be a friend or to be an enemy."

Cree Proverb

Ukrainian Verses

I wish I knew them better....
so that I could bring sense to their madness,
a soul to their sadness,
and sponsor new gladness.

Alas, I have only seen
the greed and power lust of their blood brothers,
the belligerence and bias of their predecessors,
and the landings of their conquering hordes.

I have not embraced them as near neighbors.
I have not supped with them,
or swapped stories around a campfire.
I have not joined them at an altar of praise.

I have not known their colicky, teething babies,
or their schoolboy sports legends,
their housewarming parties,
or their intimate family gatherings.

It's hard for me to relate to the raging fires,
the constant artillery barrages,
the ballistic missile threatening,
and the scenes of carnage and death.

Have I hardened my heart
to the bright yellow and royal blue banners
flying on flagpoles and emblazoned on
the doors and walls of places I pass daily?

Have I silenced my sensibilities
to the repeated hue and cry
of social media platforms, CNN, and MSNBC
the church, the charities, and the mission-minded?

Somehow, I can't make the distant whiteness work,
when my lament about how little Black lives matter here
is still so pregnant and so present
in my everyday reckonings.

Somehow, I can't hear the din of bullets
from Russian Kalashnikovs buffeting Kyiv,
over the wailing of Patrick Lyoya's mourners
in Grand Rapids and the Congo.

Lord, I want to be better at this.
I want to be more compassionate,
more connected and more conscious.
I want to love them like Christ commands.

I don't ever wish to show disdain,
for the crisis that now plagues Ukraine.
I want to scream at a despot gone insane,
whose brought real terror to the sweeping Baltic plain.

I only wish I knew them better...
so that I could bring sense to their madness,
a soul to their sadness,
and sponsor new gladness.

Confirmation

My soul looks back and wonders.

Y'all tried to bully a sister,
tried to beat her down,
tried to twist her up
like a pretzel at Aunt Annie's
in the Mall of America.
She bent...
but she wouldn't break.

Questioned her impeccable credentials.
Questioned her timely jurisprudence.
Questioned her sagacity, veracity, and ability.
She showed you unassailable tools.
She showed you she didn't suffer fools.
She showed you she could handle the duels.
She show you she was better, brighter, and wrapped tighter.
She bent...
but she wouldn't break.

Back in the day,
one SCOTUS pretender called it
"a high-tech lynching."
He was all kinda' wrong.
We call him "Uncle",
and it ain't a term of endearment.
Don't even get me started on that...
His lack of suitability for the job,
lack of sound judgment,
lack of moral fiber,
lack of discretion,
has been a clear and present danger,
for more years than a nation of laws

should ever have allowed.
Yet there he sits.

Yeah, we watched you this time too.
Y'all tried to crush her spirit,
and she rebounded...
tried to bring her to tears,
and she resounded...
tried to smear her character...
and she confounded.
She answered every bell
with dignity and class,
countered every argument
with truth, as clear as glass,
didn't lose her reason,
when you acted like an ass.
And did you ever.

But I digress...

She bent...
but she wouldn't break.

And even on a day
when a nation
should have been uniform
in its admiration,
ready to make a unified
proclamation,
that it's not about
gender or pigmentation...
Y'all ended up
showing your retardation,
stupid and foolish,
foolish and stupid.
Y'all can choose the order.

Doesn't matter anyhow.
Pride goeth before a fall...

She bent...
but she didn't break.

53 to 47.
Confirmation.
Justice is served
by God and heaven.
Like petulant boys,
you promptly took your toys,
and stormed out the room.
Partially swept by
the Democrat's broom...

But I digress.

Scotus take notice.
There's a real Sister on the way.
We're just waiting
for the swearing-in day.
Maybe Madame Justice isn't totally blind.
She must have snuck a tiny peek,
looking out for womankind.

Despite the disappointment
at the way it all went down,
we'll call it still a victory
for black, and tan, and brown...
for the us, and the U.S.
A televised revolution?
Perhaps a bar too high,
but our folks don't get nothin'
without reaching for the sky.

Ketanji Brown Jackson,
drunk fools best get sober.
Especially when
when you take your seat,
first Monday in October.

For the confirmation of Supreme Court Justice,
the Honorable Ketanji Brown Jackson,
April 7, 2022.

Ventilation

We had to get out of each other's way.
We really had nothing more to say.
We had to agree to disagree,
 so we could stop being disagreeable.

She wouldn't wear the mask.
I couldn't even ask.
She wouldn't get the shot.
I couldn't move her off the spot.

Said her freedom meant more than anything...
Wasn't gonna' let the liberals win,
wasn't gonna' cave to the do-gooders and the socialists.
Said she was a real American.

I couldn't disagree with anything more,
except...
seeing her through that horrid plate glass,
all hooked up to high-priced hoses,
chest heaving and convulsing.

I couldn't requite this
with any semblance of maternal instinct,
with any redeeming notion of choice,
any proper concept of free will,
or any legitimate definition of family values.

I could only acquiesce
to the final decision
to shut the machines off,
to let fear fade from her countenance,
and give her peace...

I could only cry a little...
Tears are a pauper's
hand-me-downs,
when what you really crave
are loving hugs and human connection.

I could only get out of her way.
I resolved to keep silence
one last time...
agreeing to disagree,
so as not to be disagreeable.

No Charges

Death shouldn't come so easy.
Peace officers on the prowl...
no knock, no warrant...no problem.
A hail of bullets,
a dead black woman...
no crime, no guilt.
In the prison of her own home,
in the privacy of her own bed,
in the quiet of pillow talk...
or sleeping while Black.
Cops on a hunch, a hint, a tip...
intent on the silent but deadly,
deadly force,
deadly result.
Lives that just don't seem to matter.
No fault, no accountability...
no charges.

Breonna Taylor...
Breonna Taylor...
Breonna Taylor...
Say her name, again.

The Hurt Locker

Have you seen what an m134 mini-gun can do
to a paddle boat on a pond?
Google it.
These armaments are no joke.
They got this stuff in concrete bunkers
and backwoods hurt lockers...
killing machines they laugh about
as they blow up stuff
to gangsta' refrains from Ice T and Snoop Dog,
or country rock riffs from Lynyrd Skynyrd
and the Charlie Daniels Band.

Hate created this.
Ain't no uncreating it.
NRA makin' real sure of that.
Gun control is an oxymoron,
grinned at by the real morons,
with an unquenchable thirst for America First,
and high-grade military ordinance.
A dozen M60's lined up on a makeshift range
somewhere in the hinterlands,
but captured in hi-def and
plastered onto 12 inch screens.
They want us to know.
They want us to see.
They want us to be afraid...
very afraid.

The hood is a target-rich environment.
We won't even stop killing each other.
They applaud our small arms fratricide.
They're gearing up for a bigger theater.
Five-O ain't even got their kind of fire-power.

They're thinking about a permanent purge.
I'm serious right now, son.
Black folks are gonna' die.

I'm watching it right now.

A hundred facebook reels
haunting my dreams...
hapless coyotes and
squealing wild pigs
caught in the cross-hairs
of high-powered long guns,
picked off like monkeys
grooming the lice
off their bush mates...
Common ritual
reinforces social structures
and communal bonds.
They've become the hate
they cultivate.
They let supremacy motivate.

New Black Panthers ain't up for this.
Bloods and Crips ain't up for this.
Gang-bangers ain't built for this.
OG's and hard-core rappers
talk a good game, but this ain't
what they signed up for.
Too many of the real fighters
locked up and locked down.
There's a reason for that.
They want us to know.
They want us to see.
They want us to be afraid...
very afraid.

The hood is a target-rich environment.
We won't even stop killing each other.
We got our own hurt lockers
and their filled with
jealousy,
and self-loathing,
and betrayal,
and a crabs-in-a-barrel mentality,
that caters to the hate...
the hate we cultivate,
the hate that separates
the few haves,
from the many have-nots.

We're just not ready for this.
But make no mistake about it.
They were born ready.
I'm serious right now, son.
Black folks are gonna' die.

They got cut-buddies in the local pd's.
They got state reps ousting the black and tan
on trumped-up policy beefs.
They got judges in their pockets.
They got super-pacs and dark money
with unchecked millions to spend,
and unfiltered venom to inject
into the veins of thirsty sheep.
They're re-writing the precinct road maps
to keep us from building consensus,
deconstructing the power of our franchise,
and silencing the voice of dissent...
in the cities and towns,
in the boroughs and counties,
in the red, blue, and purple states,
neighborhood by neighborhood.

The hurt lockers are filled
with the soiled laundry of
of our blood, sweat and tears...
Riddled by the lead bullets of
Henry rifles, and Colt pistols,
menaced by the black talons
in Glocks and Rugers and Kalashnikovs,
ambushed by high-powered Sig Sauers
and supremacist hate-speech...

A hundred IG pics and facebook reels,
happy Texas families...
at the range...
target practice
replacing Disney movies
and ice cream Sundays.
Common ritual
reinforces social structures
and communal bonds.
They've become the hate
they cultivate.
They let supremacy elevate.

And they don't care what we think...

They want us to know.
They want us to see.
They want us to be afraid...
very afraid.

seven

seven bullets in the back
is not a "get well soon" card.
Jacob Blake survived...
that's not what they intended.
we will never see proper justice,
as long as we are the hunted.
we will never feel better
about just being wounded
and left for dead,
or carted off to the ER,
and handcuffed to the bed.

New Southern Shame

Once upon a time,
a Negro boy's charred body
hung from an old oak tree
in Mr. Bartlett's field...
swung like a Quinceañera piñata, from an old oak tree
in Mr. Bartlett's field.

Once upon a time,
friends and family
and folks from far and wide
gathered to view
the burnt up "nigrah"...
that should'a known better
than getting familiar
with Mr. Bartlett's
precious daughter.

Ahhhh, but you knew different.
Knew that poor brown boy's
only crime was to be
on the wrong side of those tracks,
when a group of young white punks
were trying to have their way
with Mr. Bartlett's
precious daughter.

You knew it all.
White girl shamed...
Black boy blamed.
Darktown framed...
passions inflamed.
The white man's game,
always the same.

Once upon a time...

the silence was deafening.
You watched the mayhem
and you did not speak...
not a whimper, not a whisper, not a wish—
only forlorn glances,
shaking heads,
and wringing hands.

Later, among your familiars,
in the gardens of your forebears...
you washed your hands of
this white man's burden,
with never a nod toward
real justice for the victim.
You decried the shame of it all,
over watercress and cucumber toast points,
while you sipped sweet tea and Jack,
or perhaps a Mint Julep.

Those white-washed columns don't
hold up the Old South anymore...
no Jackson, or Davis, or Lee.
They're all Black folk now,
living on the other side of the tracks.
Jackson, Davis, and Lee...
all Black folk.
How curious.

You don't hear sirens very often,
in your wrought iron gated confines.
It's all so civil now.
Old money keeps proper folk
peaceful and detached,
from the noise
and the dirt of urban decay.

Meanwhile...

in the deep, dark hollows
of your manicured counties,
bivouacs have formed
beside the mud and cypress.
Garrisons of the new confederacy,
small gauntlets of supremacy,
demonize black, brown, and tan...
amid the military ordinance,
and militant routine.

The God you visit every Sunday,
in that oh-so-proper Baptist church...
might as well be wearing the white robe
and peaked hood of nightly terror,
so removed is he from
true redemption and agape love...
And yet the preacher
professes the golden rule,
prays from the Beatitudes,
and the Song of Songs...
every Sunday.

Once upon a time...
you had to let their people go.
Yankee interlopers
had their way
with your good ol' boys—
blue, gray, black and white,
lots of killing, so many dead...
so much left unresolved.
Guilt, debt, hate, heaven, and hell...
so much left unresolved.

Yesterday, county sheriff's men
shot and killed a Black boy,
near Mr. Bartlett's place.

His great grand-daughter
claims the man groped her
at Pike's Barbeque.
Place is always packed,
but nobody saw anything.

They chased that boy
until he couldn't run
no more.
Claim he resisted arrest,
and tried to get the deputy's gun.
No cameras or cell phones, this time...
and nobody saw anything.
Right in front of Mr. Bartlett's
wrought iron gate...
just a whisper away,
from where they hung that
other black boy,
three generations hence.

Good ol' boys use Twitter now,
and trade recipes for anarchy
on the dark web.
They hide in plain sight now...
with no hint of ongoing Southern shame.
They swear the South will rise again...
and that they won't lose the war twice.
Blue, gray, black and white
lots of killing, so many dead...
so much left unresolved.
Guilt, debt, hate, heaven, and hell...
so much left unresolved.

Old man Bartlett died ugly.
Consumption and cancer
ate him alive.

He never sought redemption.
Even though he too knew
it was the good ol' boys,
that had their way
with his precious daughter...
Come to find out
she was quite the party favor.

Scuttle-but has it
that the "all-state" QB,
blonde haired and 'Bama bound
sexed the great grand-daughter,
while his "O" line
hooted and cheered
then took the sloppy seconds.
They say she didn't mind it a bit...
didn't make no fuss at'all.

All that black boy
from the other side of the tracks knew
was that he had to run.
White girl shamed.
Black boy blamed.
Darktown framed.
Passions inflamed.
The white man's game,
is still the same.

The white man's game,
don't have no shame.

If You Kill Us All

If you kill us all,
what will it matter?
Can you then live
peaceably,
among your all-white
neighbors?

I think not.
History has shown you
to be a vengeful,
violent and voracious lot.

You will soon
set your sights
on all that you covet...
on the other side,
where his grass is greener,
and his fruit is sweeter,
and his land is more fertile.
You will trumpet your virility,
further suppress your humility,
and repress all thoughts of
humanity,
civility,
charity
and equity.

Your rich will get richer.
Your poor will grow poorer.
Class will divide.
Caste will conquer.
Fences, borders and barriers will persist.

Killing the Black seed
will not make you smarter,
will not make you gentler,
will not restore your faith,
your sanity, your purity,
or your perceived nobility.

It will only expand your avarice,
your over-reaching,
your psychoses,
and your desire to dominate someone,
or something,
or everyone...
and everything.

It is a preternatural sickness...
some caustic remnant
of ancient Viking bloodlust,
or a Germanic rubric of savagery,
born of Caucasus Mountain madness
and Slavic barbarism.
It will not solve a problem of race.
It will only hasten
the purges and cleansing of your own.
It will only hasten
a hundred new Crusades,
a thousand other final solutions,
and endless Jonestown separations.

You will never be satisfied with your lot,
your larder,
and your store.
Cult, clique
and clan
will always demand
prideful patriarchy,

frenzied feudalism,
and heinous hegemony.

History can hide,
but not deny.
Sociology can mask,
but not evade.
Facts once buried in darkness
will soon come to light
in the white heat
of a black sun...
thought successfully vanquished.

If you kill us all,
what will it matter?
The unforgiven blackness
was never your enemy.
Your true demons
live within.

Lineage

Great grand-daddies trained up wild west killers.
Grand-daddies trained up deep south shooters.
Daddies trained up new south snipers.
Old men training up young boys to hunt, to harass, to maim, and
to murder.

Go everywhere with malicious intent and seditious instincts.
Go anywhere with more and bigger guns than the local LEOs.
Go somewhere in search of Black lives that don't matter...not one bit.
Unhindered, unhurried, undeterred by thin blue lines and orange
barricades...
Unfazed by the ACLU, and the SLPC, Homeland Security, the
Justice Department, and the FBI...
Finding solace in sinful senators, and craven congressmen, and
a felonious assault on the laws of the land by
the former fool upon the hill.
Plenty of badges, benches, and bivouacs to run to and hide behind.
Plenty of complicit commentary from the NRA and Fox News Today.
More recipes for anarchy and assassination from the dark web and the
trolling twitterati.

Great grand-mamas trained up docile and demure mothers.
Grand-mamas trained up "stand by your man" daughters.
Mamas trained up loud, proud and wrong Karens.
Old women training up young girls to scream,
to shout, to foster, and to follow.
Turn a blind eye on your husbands as they indoctrinate your sons.
Turn down your gaze from your boyfriends as they bully and
berate you.
Turn the other cheek and cringe before they slap that one too...
Unrepentant, unapologetic, and undeterred by the black and blue
reminders of their complicity.

Unfazed by the hate, and hurt, and hubris forming in the fertile minds
of the children they bore...
Finding solace in Jack Daniels days, valium afternoons,
and viagra nights of gin-soaked sex and faked satisfaction...
no closets, no cover, no conscience to run to and hide behind.

Where are you in the midst of this?
What have you learned and from whom?
Why haven't you chosen better teachers?
How can your spirit abide with such rage and chaos?
How segregated are your Sundays?
What kind of Christian are you?

Great grandparents, long since graveyard dead,
still cast long shadows over the poplar tree canopy
and wrap-around porches.
Grandparents enfeebled, but solidly entrenched,
still preach the gospel of separate and unequal.
Parents still shed their hoods and robes
to blend in by day and shop at the Sam's Club.
Conflicted kids can love Jay-Z and Beyonce,
but hate every Black kid at the re-segregated school across the tracks.

Civil wars begin in the cold hearts of wild west killers.
Lynchings begin in the minds of deep south shooters.
Insurrection oozes like sweat from the pores of new south snipers.
Old malevolence hides like the iceberg, beneath the tip
of the amber waves of grain and the purple mountain's majesty.
Racist legacies have been renewed and reactivated.
The rocks have cried out.
The torch has been passed.
The cross is burning in the still of the night.
This is the curse of lineage.
This is America too.

Fast Times

He didn't go out looking to die today.
The herb was good,
so he was still a little buzzed.
It's legal though
and it came from the dispensary.
Getting high ain't supposed
to be a death sentence.
Just after sun-up...
he just wanted to clear his head
and grab some munchies
at the corner bodega,
when the police stopped him.
Yes, his speech was slurred;
and yes his eyes were a little red.
Did they have to knock him
down to the ground?
Did they have to kick
and punch and choke him?
He heard the epithets
and deadly threats,
even through the 420 haze.
He didn't resist.
He couldn't have put up
much of a fight anyway.
He posed no danger to them...
four of them,
and then four more.
Lights and sirens all around.
Guns drawn.
He posed no danger to them...
No one around.
No one saw anything.
Body-cams off...

No witnesses.
Damn.
He didn't go out looking to die today.
But they killed that boy,
graveyard dead.
Smothered him, knees and boots
on his chest, arms, throat,
and private parts.
No cell phone footage.
No conscientious objectors.
No dissenters.
No saviors.
Thin blue lines converging
to consolidate the lie,
and keep their story straight.
Said he had a knife,
waving it around in a threatening manner...
feared for their safety.
De-escalation wasn't an option.
Followed their training to the letter.
Nothing but blue to corroborate.
Bystanders got there sad and late.
Another black boy's expiration date...
racism served on a breakfast plate.
Happens more than it ever should.
Makeshift shrine of flowers and wood.
"X" marks the spot where he last stood.
That's what they call,
fast times in the hood.

From Pet to Threat

As long as I can keep you right here,
 close like a warm puppy,
 it's all good.
You don't want much.
You don't need much.
You don't ask for the other thing....
 the better thing...
 the higher thing...
You're satisfied, settled and content.

You'll chase the thing I want you to chase,
 fetch the thing I want you to fetch.
You come when I call you,
 heel when I say enough.
As long as it's about perspiration,
 and not aspiration...
 about trepidation,
 and not inspiration.
I can't have you getting a whiff of yourself.

Problem right now is,
 you want to declare some things,
 for me to be aware of some things,
 to continue to compare some things,
 to how it used to be.

Problem right now is,
 you want to change the place,
 for me to rearrange the place,
 lose some of the strange this place
 makes you feel sometimes.

That's not why we brought you here...
 why we took great pains to enslave you,

shared countless trinkets to trade for you,
colonized whole countries to contain you,
transported you across countless passages,
continents, islands and oceans.
Our only thoughts were to
captivate...
incarcerate...
emasculate...
domesticate
acculturate...
you...all of you,
to the nature of our things,
our ways,
our subjugation,
and dehumanization
from whoever you think
you're supposed to be...
from whatever you think
you can become.

We created this cruel menagerie.
We call it chattel slavery...
so that you could be the consistently obedient pet
and we could be the occasionally benevolent master,
but more regularly, the prison warden...
the vile and violent overseer,
the filthy leering rapist,
the bloodthirsty lyncher,
the malevolent mob leader,
the hateful henchman.

Every device and every debt
should have kept you from becoming a threat,
to our ways and our wishes and our whims.

Problem right now is,
you want to keep declaring things,

keep making us be aware of things,
continue to be comparing some things
to how it used to be.

Problem right now is,
you want to keep on changing the place,
to be steadily rearranging the place,
to get rid of all the strange this place
makes you feel today.

Now the puppy has become the pit bull.
The fluffy fur has become the chainmail vest.
The ears are pinned back,
and the fangs are bared.
The tail no longer wags the dog.
The lion will no longer lay among the sheep.

You know your name now.
You will no longer come,
when the master calls you the old thing,
the thing that no longer contains
who and what you've become.
You've learned to love yourself.

And it ain't no puppy love.

You're a clear and present danger
to anyone who would continue to
captivate...
incarcerate...
emasculate...
domesticate
acculturate...
you...all of you,
to the nature of our things,
our ways,

our subjugation,
and dehumanization
from whoever you think
you're supposed to be...
from whatever you think
you've now become.

--Backyards--

"All that eye and heart could own
Rich domains to roam at will
When the morning sun went down
See him on his eastern hill"

Excerpted from "The Indian" a poem written by the
Narragansett Poet Flying Squirrel, ca. 1936

A Black King in Boston

Occasionally unforgiving,
frequently unconditional,
totally unapologetic...
This was the kind of blackness
his people required,
and supported,
and saluted.

He was the angry one.
He was the one that couldn't be
pacified, assimilated,
placated, or gentrified.
He didn't yield on principle.
He didn't negotiate dishonor.
He didn't suffer fools easily.

He shouted truth to power,
no hang-dog looks,
or hat-in-hand harmonizin',
no steppin' or fetchin'.

He was a real one...
Every bit the King that Martin was.
Every bit the icon that Medgar was.
Every bit the prophet that Malcolm was.
Every bit the leader that Barack came to be.

The Mayors had to deal with him.
The local LEO's had to deal with him.
The movers and the shakers in the city
had to deal with him.
White folks, had to deal with him.

Bald head, beard and daishiki...
He came at you and he was fearless.

Folks got their popcorn,
'cause they knew there was gonna' be a show,
knew that their man was in the building,
on the streets,
at the mike.

Mel King didn't play.
He was about slowin' down gentrification.
He was about talkin' up reparations.
He was about delayin' and denyin'
the wholesale incarceration
of the boyz in the hood.

The bowtie wasn't about being cute.
The bald head wasn't about lack,
or loss, or surrender.
The dashikis and overalls
weren't about eccentricity...
no humble paeans to Afrocentricity.
This king wasn't down with style complicity.
He wore his crown with authenticity.

The city of Grove Hall,
the city of Four Corners,
the city of Mattapan Square,
the city of Dudley Station,
the city of rage and riot,
the city made chill and quiet.

Mr. King didn't play.
You know the story.
He showed the way,
no guts, no glory.
Just tell the truth,
is what he'd say.
We're gonna' settle
this business today.

You don't respect the royalty.
My life reflects my loyalty.
I can't raise up to my former length.
My cane and my chair don't steal my strength.
They're just a different staff and throne,
as I gave the city my blood and bone.

This gives the poet lines for a poem.
Boston has always been his home.
He never chose to run or roam.
Boston will always his my home.

In memoriam, with respect and admiration
to a real one, Melvin H. King, Bostonian
March 2023

Ándale

A couple of little dudes live across the street.
It's a nice family...Dominican, first time home owners.
I speak my little bit of Spanish with them occasionally.
They don't laugh or correct me.
Respect is important in both of our cultures.
We don't always find ways to love one another.

The little dudes have twin scooters.
They're not more than a year apart.
They have light brown skin like me.
In another life, they could be my sons.
I ache for them...
The scooter rides will not last forever.

Will the streets they're told to stay off of
ever treat them as equals?
Or will they always run headlong into
fences, borders, and barriers,
guns, drugs, and the justice system,
schools that don't educate brown boys well,
and ignorance that doesn't abate or age gracefully?

For now, I just watch them play.
If their ball rolls across the street,
I toss it back to them.
They run to the corner of the yard, yelling "ándale!"
I see them clearly.
The innocence and joy they represent
is unmistakable, even in a language,
that is for the most part, foreign to me.

I cannot make you understand
how much their innocence and joy

speaks to me.
I cannot make you understand
how much I ache for them.

Screen Saver

Some mornings,
before I can make my actual petition known
to my 14-inch window on the world,
Bing takes me to places I did not ask to go...
the Hoggar Mountains in Algeria,
waist deep in geometrically carved sand dunes
and jagged peaks of foreboding antiquity.
I am riveted to the truth of
God the craftsman,
God the architect,
and God the comedian.

This place is ridiculous
in the calculus
of its dimension,
ludicrous
in the arid impossibility
of its isolation,
and hilarious
in the joyous revelation
of its visual splendor...

My screen flickers and changes,
as the desktop imagery
shifts to icons of industry
and reminders of the daily grind.

No doubt, tomorrow's waking portal
will take me to some aboriginal Incan ruins
at Cusco or Macchu Piccu...
some epic castellation along the shores of the Rhine...
or a white-washed fishing village
in Andalusia or North Cornwall...

All beautiful antiquities,
among the trappings of man...
but hardly comparable to what
God, the Master Builder
has wrought,
in the searing heat
of a desert,
where even angels
may fear to tread.

Home Makeover Happiness

Chip and Joanna got it on lock,
a beautiful home on each Waco block.
The copper gutters and those antique shutters,
the homeowner screams at each feature Jo utters.

The best damn homes in the Lone Star state,
by a builder and his designing mate...
He lives for thrill of demo day.
She prefers a gentler way.

He's about houses with seven gables.
She gets Clint to make her some tables.
They turned their attention to the social side,
where Twitter and facebook and IG collide.

Now their Magnolia Enterprise
expands DIY to super-size,
that made in Texas way of life,
carved up the pie with a Bowie knife.

The tree was perfect before they cut it.
Now what matters is how they strut it.
Paint and flooring, tile and glass...
Jo likes shiplap and lots of green grass.

Open concepts and master suites,
double vanities and bamboo sheets,
a butler's pantry with built in hutch...
the first-time buyer will love it so much.

Home makeover happiness,
a story with every home they bless...
Chip and Joanna do it up right.
Like Motel Six, they leave on the light.

Haiku in the Hood

Ice comes from the 'fridge.
Fudgsicles, back in the day...
Nutty Buddies too.

It's a Black thing, yo.
No you can't be down with this.
Get your own Jordans.

It don't take all that.
shouting, dancing in the aisles...
Y'all need to sit down.

Stereotype yes,
but watermelon, come on.
We all dig on that.

Be here at ten Bruh!
We at the spot by midnight.
Bring lots of singles!

It's legal home slice.
But don't get it twisted, son.
They'll still lock us up.

I need my money.
They done shut off my 'lectric.
Natty Grid don't play!

Mystic River Melancholy

The freshly coiffed Boho boys
make real estate videos
extolling the finer virtues of West Medford,
and life along the Mystic River.

Maybe they're new money kids or Tufts grads
that don't know the rich history of the village.
They do have a sense that
this is a minor Mecca for ex-city dwellers,
flush with IPO cash, NFT windfalls, or Bitcoin early adoptions...
a new gentry that wants to be landed
for their dogs,
and their Range Rovers,
and their wine tastings,
and the next generation of trust fund babies.

The would-be property princes
have a target market.
The Youtube appeal is slick and shiny...
classic Americana
with a side of Sushi,
or a vente mocha latte.

They have no idea of
what used to be.
They know what the next wave
wants to see.

They want to see
the bikes, the hikes,
and their kids on trikes.
They want to post pics,
that will get lots of likes.

They want to see
the flowering trees,
and the birds and the bees.
Their high-rise havens,
had none of these.

They want to see
if they can grow something green
in a backyard garden,
beyond the green that's growing
in their bulging bank accounts.

Newsflash...
Designer overalls and Doc Martens
do not a farmer make.
No worries...
Whole Foods has gone 100% organic,
with a great selection of finely-curated herbs and spices.

I know that this sounds like resentment.
Resignation frequently does.
But when the private boat clubs
bookend the public beach,
and the abutters don't want loud, unruly Dominicans
descending on their hillsides for beachfront parking,
well...
what's a brother from the Ville to think?

My daddy taught me how to fish here...
not much more than eels and sunfish in the water then,
but it felt like legacy,
and we were happy to have it.

They didn't really want us at their beach back then either,
but we were mighty in our minority.
We didn't want to fight folks,

but the lake wasn't exactly pristine,
so why begrudge it to anybody?

We could walk that half mile,
or ride our stingray bikes down there
and feel connected to the small waves and the gentle wake.
We could wonder about the kayakers,
and the canoe paddlers,
the colorful sun fishers,
occasional scullers,
and the ubiquitous motor boaters.
We could dream a little dream
about owning a dinghy and a trawling engine,
and making a few waves of our own.

Don't get me wrong...
I love the new fish ladders
and the intrepid herring counters,
the trout infusion,
the bald eagle sightings,
and the focus on environmental sustainability.
Thing is...
they love it too...
and they can afford to pay for it.

One point four mil'
for Queen Dorothy Elizabeth Tucker's old homestead.
It should have been a historical landmark.
Instead, it's yet another preview of coming attractions.

Meanwhile, the sleepy little Nubian hamlet,
has released its black and brown patina
to the inexorable tug of real property values,
and the dying off of the old guard.

Mine is the last generation
that knew about the first three streets...

Arlington, Lincoln and Jerome,
that knew about the little store,
the old Shiloh Baptist,
and the library, in the fire station.

Mine is the last generation
that knew about Charlie Booker and the Bruins...
the five fighting Phillips brothers,
Uncle Buddy's postal command,
Doc Kountze's blue books,
Faucenia and Evelyn's salon,
and exactly why it's called Dugger Park.

So many firsts.
So much history.
So little time to savor and to save,
to preserve and to pass on.
So many departures,
and so few arrivals
of the black and the brown and the tan.

Meanwhile, the developers mostly have their way.
The Spanish day laborers tear it down
and build it back up...
Like Lee Majors in the Six Million Dollar Man,
they have the technology.
They can make them better than they were...
better, stronger, faster.

Condos and townhouses...toney and trendy...
Out with the old.
In with the new.
Wash, rinse, and repeat.

Meanwhile, the freshly coiffed Boho boys
make real estate videos,
extolling the finer virtues of West Medford
and life, along the Mystic River.

Red Line Reflections

We haven't left the station yet.
The bell is ringing like a banshee's screech...
and the doors slowly close.

I count roughly thirty riders...
all kind of folk,
from day laborers to defense lawyers.
Everybody's got their cell/laptop/tablet out.

Everybody's inside the tech bubble.
An occasional sip of Dunkin' joe lifts the chin.
No Starbucks' cups on this run.
Seems like the only piece of common ground,
save the I-phone ubiquity

New riders embark at each next stop.
Hoodies, high heels and track suits
meet all-star high tops and cowboy boots...
lots of little white earbuds, Dr. Dre Beats,
and big Bose noise-cancellers.

I wonder what they're listening to,
definitely not each other.
Blank stares at tiny screens,
or animated exclamations,
in what should be private conversations...
I hear the f-bombs drop,
but no one seems to be affected.

I need to get to my stop.
I need more humanity and less technology now.
I need a purge and a cleanse and maybe a hug.

I need to take the mask off,
and not feel so vulnerable
to the heavy breathing, sneezes, and throat clearing.

This ride is both invasive and isolating.
Dude is so close to me,
yet totally oblivious to my existence.
He smells like burnt curry.
My nose is itching and my eyes water a bit.
Personal space is a distant shore.

It's really crowded now.
I can't see any of the six doors.
Makes my neck feel hot.
My stop is next.
I'm 'a get off this train
and ask Sire to play the Hallelujah Chorus.
I know I couldn't do this every day.

I'm not crazy about driving;
But it seems the lesser of two evils...
No heavy breathing, sneezes, or throat clearing, save my own...
and no burnt curry smell.

Tomorrow it's my own bubble,
93 North, bumper to bumper...
and brake lights all the way.

But no one in my face and no mask.
WHRB and the Jazz Spectrum soothes the spirit.

Red Line Ruins

Got on the Red Line at Park Street...
tired, hungry, and stressed.
Long nasty scrum
on my way to the daily grind...
Nothing went right,
late for the presentation
and wrong damn slides
on the Power Point...
Fighting back tears,
'cause this was supposed to be my ticket to the next level.
Best thing I can say about it, d-o-n-e "done!"

Approaching Downtown Crossing
and the train is screeching on the rails.
I want to screech right along with it.
No, seriously....
I'm in a downward spiral.
Down to South Station.
Down to Broadway.
Down to Andrew.
I looked up at JFK.
I always do...no matter what.

Maybe because I'm out of the tunnel.
Out of the dark
and into the light of the sun,
or the lights of the city,
beyond Congress and State and Federal
and Downtown Crossing.
We in Dorchester, yo.
We back in the hood.
Ain't gotta front.
Ain't gotta switch it up.

Six sets of identical doors,
and she had to walk through mine...
shine through mine,
be fine through mine,
like new wine through mine.

So smitten,
like a baby kitten...
I knew I'd been bitten.

Eyes met...
like it was kismet,
like winning a prop bet,
like paid off school debt.
like a good, cheap sublet.
Oooh, this place is really nice.
That cake, I'd like to have a slice.

Sat down right next to me,
just as love texted me,
just as her eyes inspected me,
just as fate expected me
to say something.
Dude, just say something.
Your stop is coming up.

Shouldn't have been so hard,
to hand the girl my business card.
The doors opened so very fast.
I couldn't make the magic last.
She'll never call; the die is cast.

Another bad ride
on these sucky Boston trains,
a brother's busted pride
on these sucky Boston trains,

a chance at bliss got swept aside
on these sucky Boston trains.
Romance just suffered homicide,
on these sucky Boston trains.

The Wasteland

My wife is a
this is busted,
this is broken,
this won't work now,
kind of spouse.

I find that stuff's
in disrepair...
in every room
of my house.

It's fortunate that I'm patient,
not a "honey, I'm the man!"
She's quick to put
what might be saved
in a trash bag,
or waste can.

And so we do
a marriage dance,
with some accommodation.
I must now anticipate
most of her frustration.

Brothers, if you're contemplating
your own situation,
here's a bit of sage advice,
to move past aggravation.

If she claims it's broken,
just smile and let it go.
Buying her another one,
will make you her he-ro.

If it's busted in her mind,
that must guide your hand...
Remove this awful denizen
from your calm and peaceful land.

If she says it doesn't work,
please don't hesitate.
Drop it like bad habit,
to try and please your mate.

Don't default to shouting out,
"No dear, that's just wasting!"
The bile will move up in her craw,
and that's what she'll be tasting.

Please find no delight
in exercising manly might,
except to carry this janky stash,
and toss it in the household trash.

New England Song

The still waters of your mystical lakes,
gilded with the copper, bronze and gold rush
of Autumn's tonal onslaught...
it beckons poetry...
words of adoption and affirmation.

With a Mississippi pedigree
and a native son's soul,
this northern sensibility
that finds compatibility
with a Southern spirituality...
sometimes shocks the core of me.

Vermont snows beckon,
and the humbled novice skier
hunkers down in the quaint cabin...
Hot chocolate nights and s'mores communions
warm the frozen fingers with snap, crackle, and pop.

Five Forks in the Spring...
my honorary Chinese Pó Po's farm,
is the closest I can come to Uncle Lincoln's place.
But there are no chickens, pigs, or milk cows...
no smokehouse ribs, catfish fries, or crawdad boils either.

No, these fields grow tulip landscapes,
vibrant dahlia dreams,
and long-stemmed wedding roses.
Floral seasons occasionally give way
to sweet corn, fat tomatoes and fuzzy melons too.

Cape Cod summers
on the Vineyard and

at Hyannisport,
mesmerize beyond
Chocktaw cheeks and Biloxi beignets.

Full-bellied fried clams,
chilled lobster rolls,
and creamy, steamy "chowdah"
are essential reminders
of the tasty treasures
in the Atlantic's near harbors.

The fall returns with the rough-hewn stone walls,
the ones Mr. Frost said "make good neighbors".
City dwellers make pilgrimages to the country orchards.
Jonagold, Cortland and Empire apples shout "pick me."
Golden brown chilled juice jugs shout "drink me."
Once a year cinnamon and sugar-crusted cider donuts shout "devour me."

Southern heritage embraces South Shore sensibilities.
Plymouth Harbor is bright and breezy.
The autumn leaves begin to fall.
Harvest festivals announce final fruits.
Halloween haunts with costumed high jinx.
Corn stalk mazes meet ghouls, goblins, and ghosties.

New England's song is a Taylor-Diamond reprise...
a folksy Baby James and Sweet Caroline tease,
a Patti Page love affair with "Old Cape Cod",
a "Mystic River" soundtrack with an Arthur Fiedler nod.

"Winter, Spring, Summer or Fall...
all you have to do is call."
Son of Southern shores...this is how it stands...
Missituk realities are now your native sands.

Cali rockers said it best
in their grungy poem...
"I love that dirty water,
Boston, you're my home."

Oh yes, I love that dirty water,
New England, you're my home.

Ninety Says

How did I get here? I can't really say.
I've lost so many along the way.

Some say clean living...some call it grace.
For ninety-plus years, I've been in this place.

I've come through many toils and snares.
I've weathered storms, concerns, and cares.

Yet still, I'm standing, less straight and tall.
But I've gotten back up, after every hard fall.

I've raised my children as best I could.
It's nice to see them doing some good.

I guess that I should take a rest,
and smell the roses. I've been so blessed.

Nine-plus decades, I hope I've learned,
to love the wrinkles that I have earned.

I hope I remember the bridges I've crossed,
the miles I've traveled, and what the toll cost.

I pray I respect the roads I've gone down...
all the tears, each smile, and every frown.

I know that time is chasing me.
Another ten years, I may not see.

But I stopped running long ago.
I let the river have its flow.

Now there's time for celebration,
as I have reached a distant station.

How did I get here? It's hard to say.
I passed so many along the way.

I may be sad, but I don't blame,
the author of this crazy game.

I've learned to count it all as joy,
something that trouble can't destroy.

And though it's not attached to fame,
I have my family's honest name.

This victory I will surely claim.
I saw the target and took good aim.

So, even as they change the game.
The picture shines within the frame.

For the West Medford Community's "Nonagenarians"
September, 2022

--Marvels--

"Seek the ways of the eagle, not the wren."

Omaha Proverb

Her Name Is Grace

I know a spirit; her name is Grace.
I've not beheld a more sweet face.

I've never seen her sour mood,
only her pleasant attitude.

She is a source of salt and light,
from earliest dawn 'til black midnight.

She does her Father's bidding well,
and finds new mercies with each bell

Extending favor hand to hand...
she's blessing folks throughout the land.

To see her stopping by my door,
I couldn't ask for any more.

Her name is Grace, the hope of man,
the treasure of the Master's plan.

March of the Dragons

See the Gentle Dragons on parade.
Oh what a mighty sound they made,
like lion cubs wrestling in the shade.
See the Gentle Dragons on parade.

See the Gentle Dragons at the park,
ready, set, go...now on your mark.
Playing like puppies, hear them bark.
See the Gentle Dragons at the park.

Now the Gentle Dragons have their lunch.
All kinds of treats they grab and munch.
They really love grapes in a juicy bunch.
Now the Gentle Dragons have their lunch

Wacky Wednesday comes and oh what fun.
Pajamas and dress-up for everyone...
waffles and syrup, can I have some?
Don't be late, or you won't get none.

Miss Joelle knows just what to do,
at this happy, playful children's zoo.
Parents work in the classroom too.
Miss Joelle has an awesome crew.

On fun holidays, we get a treat,
and hear the thump-thump of dragon feet.
You sing to the old folk, sounds so good...
Gentle Dragons in the neighborhood.

When summer comes, they squeal with joy,
bathing suits on each girl and boy.
Everyone loves the sprinkler's spray.
This is the best part of their day.

Every year a Dragon graduates.
It's hard to leave his pre-school mates.
The moms will arrange some good play dates,
and new dragons come right through the gates.

See the Gentle Dragons on parade,
marching back from the trip they made.
Tuckered out from the games they played,
hopin' for cookies and lemonade.

For the Gentle Dragon Pre-school of West Medford, MA
September, 2022

Garden of Peace

1

In ancient writings, it is said,
"Healing is the children's bread."
We tarry in this quiet space,
to feel the very soul of grace.
We walk between each garden stone,
to gain that peace we call our own.

Among the green and gray and brown,
there hides a smile for every frown.
There dwells a balm for every hurt,
in rock-hewn paths and simple dirt.
Within the maze of human pain,
a new perspective we may gain.

Bring your cares and sorrows nigh.
Make a plea and solemn sigh.
Set your spirit at sweet ease,
as you walk, or from your knees.
You may move beyond despair,
God transcends the small and bare.

2

Soul to soul, and heart to heart...
within this space, may journeys start
to unwrap coils of stress and rage,
and loose compassion from its cage,
to bring each spirit into hope,
and give each human strength to cope.

At dawn's first light, or sunset's glow,
let your heartbeat soften and slow.
Let your troubled mind be calm.

Recite a little peaceful psalm.
Perhaps embrace a meditation,
within each circle's undulation.

A maze created for humankind,
not class, or race, and color-blind...
Leave the madness beyond the arch.
This isn't a place to angrily march.
There will be another day,
for social cause to have its say.

3

Hatred has no harbor here.
This labyrinth is free from fear.
The walls will never fence you in.
The truth requires no hype or spin.
Take a moment and breathe in deep.
The maze will comfort as you weep.

The ripple of the Mystic stream
at river's edge evokes a dream.
And yet the flow is with us still.
It leads this poet to ink and quill.
These paths may twist with every stone.
Find a road to make your own.

The artist imagines a safe enclave,
an open space that Medford gave
to all its people, from near and far,
to contemplate each cloud and star.
And now the writer takes his pen,
to say to all, remember when.

Adapted for the dedication of the
Mystic Meditation Labyrinth
Riverbend Park, Medford, MA
April 29, 2023

The Good Sister

The best thing about the good sister
are her hands...
They're steady and confident.
They're soft and welcoming.
They exhibit a calm tenacity.
They're filled with skilled dexterity.
They never take what they don't earn.
They always teach what we need to learn.

The best thing about the good sister
is her smile.
It's toothy and wide.
It's an invitation to conversation.
It's the charm that attracts and beguiles.
It's the bridge that crosses the miles.
It never sucks the air in disgust.
It always opens a door of trust.

The best thing about the good sister
is her laugh.
It's bubble up from the center of her soul.
It's resonates from the core of her humanity.
It's colorful and liberating.
It's visceral and vibrating.
It never fails to break the ice.
It always leads to something nice.

The best thing about the good sister
is her gaze.
It penetrates the darkness.
It always looks toward the light.
It draws you into her spirit.
It draws you out of the storm.

It never glares in condemnation.
It ever beams with expectation.

The best thing about the good sister
is her love.
It covers her people zealously.
It shelters her people jealously.
It embraces her people tenderly.
It repels spite and hate and enmity.
It never judges, or unfairly binds.
It leads to amazing grace of all kinds.

The best thing about the good sister
is her faith.
It governs her actions consistently.
It builds up her walk with resiliency.
It grapples with every disparity.
It looks to the Father for clarity.
It never throws in the towel, too early.
It triumphs in the end, most surely.

The very best thing about the good sister
is her heart.
It beats with a measured insistency.
It hopes with a treasured transparency.
It gives with remarkable charity.
It looks to avoid all vulgarity.
It never screams "show me the proof"!
It always says yes to the genuine truth.

Dawna Jones was ever the good sister.
Steady hands.
Big smile.
Great laugh.
Deep gaze.
Real love.

Righteous faith.
Giving heart.

She never let us down...never.
She always picked us up...always.

Dawna Jones is the good sister.
good beyond her gifts...
good beyond her goals...
good beyond her grace...
the good sister...
Always and forever.

Adapted and dedicated to the memory of Dawna L. Jones, MD
Fisk University, Class of 1980
February 12, 1959 – December 17 2022

Four Limericks for My Brothers in Fisk

There once were two brothers called Jack;
and this is historical fact...
One would procrastinate.
One would never be late...
when we Fiskites said "yo, holler back."

There once was a Brother called Kirk.
In the darkness he sometimes would lurk.
He had Texas-tall dreams,
saddle-bags full of schemes,
and the juice to make all of it work.

There once was a Brother called Terry,
who made campus life proper and merry.
He would skate cross the yard,
then write like the Bard,
turning up an occasional sherry.

There once was a Brother called Boston.
He wasn't from Memphis or Austin.
From the Dorchester hood,
this great statesman made good,
and never a country was lost in.

Dedicated to my friends from the Yard, Reginald D. Jackson, Reggie Jackson, A. Kirk Williams, Alonzo L. Fulgham, and me, Terry E. Carter... Fisk Forever!

Reginald J. Reflections

I could not tell this story
with ten-thousand chosen words.
I would not have the adjectives,
the nouns, or all the verbs.

And yet your cache of photographs
captures every smile,
recounting each reunion
with elegance and style.

Each picture boldly goes,
where we've all gone before,
the portals of the chapel
and Jubilee's sacred door.

Doc Collins babies so sublime...
The ladies of Pi are mighty fine...
Omega punch is killer juice...
Folks on the yard and getting loose.

Later they'll grab a big Ed's fish,
every old school Fiskite's wish.
The oval calls to each alum
to stroll, or step, and have big fun.

Homecomings have a flavor.
You serve it with such flair.
Remembering each queen and king,
your camera takes us there.

Fiskite sons and daughters true,
each class is honor bound...
to sing a song of gold and blue,
and march on hallowed ground.

Your camera's old school rolls,
are perfect in their tins.
And later chemistry reveals
the pride of darker skins.

Who would think a sonnet
could rightly tell this tale
of Reginald J's reflections
along this treasured trail?

Fisk University's iconic Jubilee Hall, Nashville, TN
Photo courtesy of Reginald D. Jackson, Fisk '82
© *May 2022, all rights reserved.*

Black Diamonds Rise

What is the measure of our worth?
In truth, it lies buried in Mother Earth...
pressed beneath eons of hurt and pain,
molded by pressurized scorn and shame.

How do such facets achieve their glow?
Are the secrets interred in the mines below?
Or do dark oceans have a deeper flow,
bodies dragged down by sin's undertow,
in the squalor of ships, laid out row by row.
Do only the prophets and griots know?

Carats of black and brown and tan...
mined for gold by the slaver's hand,
culled to satisfy white demand,
forged and formed to work foreign land.

So much luster covered with filth,
that never acknowledges how much they built.
So much shine eradicated.
Glorious histories violated.
Family legacies decimated.
Tribal loyalties devastated.
Echoes of chains reverberated.
Millions of live gems excavated.
The sparkle of spirit terminated.

The wealth of the maker's primal nations
stolen for untold generations...
the province of trusts and incorporations
that fight, tooth and claw, against reparations...
a thousand daily manifestations
that speak to the lie of emancipations.

From Caribbean suns to Amazon shade,
America's promises still evade...
Still promote the false ideal,
that only the white stones have appeal.
So now we declare, and yes decree
the season of synchronicity.
Let the planets and fates align,
to move us past the grim design...
to shout that gardens of anthracite,
have pressed beyond translucent white,
and set the stage for onyx stones
that celebrate our darker tones.
Now ripe with black and brown and tan,
we cultivate a lustrous plan.

From the blessed belly of Mother Earth,
we are nobility by our birth...
navigating the globe's full girth,
proving the measure of our worth,
showing the last shall be the first,
as blessings quench the victor's thirst.
Our ancestors toiled, bled and died,
to see our fortunes multiplied,
crystallized as precious jewels...
not to serve as common fools.

Now in healthy self-respect,
we'll conquer our demons of self-neglect.
We'll guard the lives we must protect...
and be the light we must project.

Black diamonds...sparkling in the sun,
each gem brilliant, every one...
not shiny pebbles cast aside,
but beautiful vessels of flawless pride,
hardened by history's harsh report,
now, our destiny we must court.

Black diamonds...formed by nature's hand,
each brother, a king in high demand...
not social pariahs or castaways,
but leading lights to brighter days,
cut to exhibit the finest trace,
of God the Father's perfect grace.

Twenty-Four Titans

They were our people,
the pulpit and the steeple...
O.G. Phillips, standing strong,
in God's house, at the appointed hour—
come to the corner of Holton and Bower.

City, State, and community,
always a purpose and a plan—
an attitude saying, "Yes we can"...
Wally Kountze
was that kind of man.

Our people...

Unique and so appealing,
a hand-rubbed, sand-finished ceiling—
fresh paint on a bedroom wall,
new tile in a bathroom stall...
Varnie Carter did it all.

Madeleine Dugger found her groove.
She made public schooling move,
even when white folks didn't approve.
The schools became a better place
for children with a darker face.

A Medford Firefighter...
Frankie Booker took control.
ascending up the fire pole—
first Black man to join the ranks
of hoses, trucks and water tanks.

Can you hear those drums?
The high hat sizzles

and a tight snare hums.
Alan Dawson led the band—
the master in command.

To protect and yes to serve...
with iron will and nerve—
a strong and quiet giant,
in blue serge and gleaming gold bars...
Rudy Smith earned those shining stars.

Faucenia Booker too...
coiffing the ladies with just the do,
to keep the men folk home—
not too many brothers roam.
She was the first with a shop of her own.

Hear the piano tinkle...
teaching beyond old age's wrinkle.
Generations learned their lessons well,
while in the sway of Ms. Adele.
Did you hear the bell?

It tolls for thee too...our people!

"Doc" Kountze told the story
of Medford's chocolate glory.
Touring the Ville on that old Schwinn bike...
before the days of a "facebook like"—
we had heroes too.

A million balls would cross the net.
Some would land in the Mystic, wet.
He never yelled at his own,
a patient and encouraging tone—
the tennis coach, Cleedie Rhone.

Train up a child every single day.
That was her kind and motherly way.
Ma' Whit...yeah, but say it right—
Milbur Whitaker, shining light...
called the Ville her home.

Sons and heirs of the slaver's tally,
who made their home in the Mystic Valley...
teachers, soldiers, and heroes galore—
from the Community Center to the Little Store.
Our people...

Our people...remember?

Twenty-four, so brave and bold...
These are stories that must be told.
Other sons will have their day.
Other daughters will have their say.
Reflect on these, who paved the way...
our local history, here to stay.

Walter Isaacs made sports the tool
that brown boys ran to after school,
showed them first the Golden Rule...
fielding grounders and catching flies,
under Mystic Valley skies.

Norma Jeffers led her girls,
from merit badges to proms and pearls,
from planting flowers to pressing curls.
The Girl Scout life was good to all—
before the cell phone, IG, and the mall.

Did your letters arrive on time?
Buddy Clayton, in his prime,
back when a stamp just cost a dime,
the local Postal Service chief...
He put a stamp on our belief.

Titans, don't you understand...
men and women built to command.

Judge Jackson always read the signs,
jurisprudence and a probing mind...
with compassion of that special kind.
She never left a child behind...
justice, neither deaf, nor blind.

Dorothy Elizabeth Tucker—revered...
many hurdles adroitly cleared.
danced straight through her ninety-fifth year.
She knew how to shift the atmosphere...
inspired those who lived down here.

Mother, mentor, molder of men,
scouting lead in the Ville's own den...
training the boys in 428,
to be prepared and elevate,
Phyllis Douglas, kept it straight!

Neighborhood sons and daughters, true...
citizens Black—red and white and blue.

Conrad Sharpton's velvet glove,
summoned souls to gospel love...
songs that beckoned heaven above.
Played that Hammond B-3, too...
lifted the Lord for me and you.

Our streets reached literary heights,
griots and scribes, talent that writes.
Parables lead to peaceful nights...
setting a tone, describing the scene,
the wordsmith, Mr. Oscar Greene.

The broom and the mop, the shovel and rakes...
a quiet giant near Mystic Lakes,
hardly ever took a break.
Herbert Adams, the Ville's caretaker,
a humble servant, the Center's home-maker.

Evelyn Tyner had a simple goal.
She made West Medford, her heart and soul...
embraced a calling and played her role.
She taught us lessons of courage and choice.
She gave her daughters that same proud voice.

Pieces of Medford's history,
no longer shrouded in mystery.

Calvin Lindsay's business tally,
flats for rent in the Mystic Valley.
Homefolk saw their fortunes rally.
A handshake often sealed the deal,
for Caribbean folk who made an appeal.

Our people...

Who taught Shiloh to sing like those hymns?
Cecily Dean, in those tortoise shell rims—
a shining light that never dims,
made the chorus sound so sweet,
with this notice, my song's complete...

Medford giants for you to know.
Twenty-four Titans in a row...
Still more stories may unfold,
for a Brown-skinned Poet
with a pen of gold.

Dedicated to 24 community legends and icons of the historic
West Medford (MA) African-American neighborhood,
June 2022.

Three Limericks for Oscar G.

There was an old salt of the 'hood...
who knew about cats pretty good.
You must change their litter,
or they'll become bitter,
and not poop in places they should.

A Rabbi met a young priest...
alone at a loud wedding feast.
Please won't you dine
at this table of nine.
The bread's made with Catholic yeast.

Two brothers got into a fight...
over how to make barbeque right.
Said the one to the other,
don't you make it like mother,
or no one will eat it tonight.

I Came for the Stories...

I came for the stories,
of how you built this place...
from the entrails,
from the dregs,
from the unwashed and the unwanted...
the only piece of the city
they'd let you have.
But you built it...
with pine and pegs and poles and persistence,
with the beauty of duty
and the substance of faith.

I came for the stories
of the heroes,
and the unheralded.
of the legacy makers,
and the territory takers,
of the boundary shakers,
and the barrier breakers...
the first ones to do
the big thing,
the bold thing,
the forbidden, the unfamiliar, the courageous thing.

I came for the stories...
The ones you saved for your children
and their children and their children...
Anansi's stories...
Shaka Zulu's stories...
Sheba's stories...
Hannibal's stories...
Toussaint's stories...
Sojourner's stories...

Malcolm, Marcus,
Martin and Medgar's stories.
Epic, heroic and tragic truth,
of how we came over...
and what we've overcome.

I came for the stories...
all of them, lost, stolen, or strayed.
Because history
can't be real for me,
can't reveal to me,
can't appeal to me...
without showing
the black
and the brown
and the tan.
White-washing so clearly
all critical race theory,
just tells me we are nearly,
erasing a past
we will pay for dearly.

I came for the stories,
only poets can tell...
magical tales that cast a spell,
living water from the griot's well,
distant drumming and a faraway bell,
the sea's reply in a Queen Conch shell,
the salted air as the billows swell.
An archangel triumphs, a demon fell.
Giants flee from where Davids dwell,
lest they drown in a deepening stell.
Legion is vanquished and sent back to hell.
The riot ends with a mournful yell.
The ode is recorded, from district to dell.

I came for the stories...
and I will not leave.
As I am beseeching
beyond my own reaching,
for all you are teaching,
the sermons you're preaching,
where black knows no bleaching...
of borders we're breaching,
as hatred is leaching,
and rage is screeching,
for love's impeaching.

I came for the stories.
I came for the stories.
I came for the stories.

--Songs--

"The words of God are not like the oak leaf which dies and falls to earth, but like the pine tree which stays green forever."

Mohawk Proverb

And the Melody Lingers On

Was it a night is Tunisia,
or some other song...
that kept the melody
lingering on?

Something some master
of jazz may have played...
captured the people,
and all of them stayed.

A maiden voyage,
expansive and new
surrounded by rhythm,
harmonically true.

Mesmerizingly,
altered the senses...
broke down the barriers—
mended the fences.

Honeyed with baritone,
leveled with bass...
a lilting saxophone
quickens the pace.

The dolphins dance
in oceans of blue,
and the sweetest romance
floats into view.

According to Ella,
the night has a peace.
Yet history sweeps,
and the romance must cease.

Stoked by the storms
of an Arab spring,
that night has become
a turbulent of thing.

The ages-old passions
of Berbers and Moors,
Muslims and Christians,
religion and wars...

Now revolution
has boiled the moon.
The melody swelters,
as patriots swoon.

Could Parker and Miles
have gotten it wrong?
Have Art Blakey's rhythms
mistaken the song?

Did Dizzy's trumpet
blare out a rhythm,
that couldn't contain
an ages-old schism?

Did a Night in Tunisia
get it wrong
in making
the classic master's song?

And yet, the great ones
genuflect,
to play the tune
with great respect.

A Night in Tunisia,
that jazzy icon...

and the melody
lingers on.

The song remains
a jazz bon-bon...
and the melody
lingers on.

A Night in Tunisia
beckons the dawn...
and the melody
lingers on.

Thelonious Assault

You were the mystic and the mage,
with every scribble on each lined page...
so deadly serious at that bench,
with eyes ablaze and teeth in clench.

Tones that spin discordant perfection,
harmonic twists in every reflection...
what is the meaning of all this scatter,
as you summon rhythmic anti-matter?

Why must you rage and violently pound
each key to achieve such a potent sound?
Reveling in a Cerulean funk,
you were the least obedient Monk.

Sometimes you'd wax melodic and quiet.
Then you'd revert to the din of a riot...
every chord with a stranglehold,
on conventional music's centerfold.

A bit of the Duke's panache and style,
with James P. Johnson's strident guile...
yours was the most ambitious spirit.
In every bar, the night can hear it.

The grand piano majestically sits.
It has no sense of the crimes it commits.
It tolerates explosive bits
of cosmic slop, as the maestro sits.

In a soft felt fez or a pork pie hat,
you were a different kind of cat...
fingers like Harlem stickball bats,
scurrying quick like tenement rats,

over those keys while the saxophone scats,
over those keys while the drummer pats,
over those keys with sharps and flats,
while the bass man thumbs out welcome mats,
in front of the door of Handy and Fats,
real conversation, not idle chats.

Wed to the notes like a pretty young wife,
jazz piano brought back to life,
the music made to cut like a knife.
Skipping chords in dissonant strife,
never to march like a drum and fife,
with crackling sparks, your soul was rife.

Yet, waves of sickness embraced your spirit.
The music allowed you to hardly hear it.
Oceans of darkness and you didn't fear it.
A constant hurdle, we watched you clear it.

Or rather we listened in special awe,
as camels buckled with every straw,
you piled on top of harmonic law,
as bop and stride made doubters thaw.
You'd soon succumb to a tragic flaw,
and be undone by depression's claw.

So still the vinyl adorns the platter,
as we revel in musical anti-matter,
Madame Pannonica's lilting splatter,
'Round Midnight with a truly mad hatter.

Solitude embraces a tortured soul,
that scales the peaks of an opposite pole...
Through a Thorazine haze that takes its toll,
and still the maestro maintains control.

The Steinway bursts in dynamic tone,
and yet the madness won't leave him alone.
The abbott cowers and runs to pray,
as the musical friar prepares to slay.

The Steinway engages in mythical work,
while legions of demons quietly lurk...
ready to take the altar away...
to assault the Monk, as we hear him play.

Haiku Divas

Sade is carved from
amber and alabaster.
Beauty has a sound.

Lady sings the blues...
She has a right to lament.
Y'all were not her friends.

Roberta can't come.
Her affliction is too strong.
The old songs remain.

Sassy's gonna' croon
and Hawk's band is in the house.
Jazz is being served.

Leontyne's priceless...
costumed in satins and lace,
operatic chills.

The gospel's true love
presents the amazing grace...
Marian's great praise.

Brown Girl at the Cello

For a moment I blinked at what I was seeing,
this chocolate hint of a Renaissance being...
My ears abruptly filled with sound,
that made my senses rise, spellbound.

Was it a wistful wail or a spectral moan?
Was it borrowed, or was it her own?
As she brought her bow across those strings,
it made me reflect on a thousand things...
of how our people persevered,
a race at once, reviled and revered.

As her fingers danced, so flowing and light,
it made me recall the perilous flight,
across the sea to freedom's beacon,
to the flame of liberty we've been seeking.

The voicings of that hourglass frame,
removed the fear, the hurt and shame.
It led us away from racial scorn.
It led us away from hate forsworn.
It led us away from love forlorn.
It led us away to places where grace is born.

The soul at peace is how it settles...
no thorns, no briars, no stinging nettles.
Was it a siren's song in the dead of night,
or the distant horizon beckoning bright?
As she brought her bow across those strings,
the spirit moves and her cello sings.

I watched a little girl gasp in wonder,
and knew in my heart, the spell she was under.

I thought I would weep at her earnest glance...
The instrument's melody made her dance.
New confidence born in this tiny frame,
whose life will never be the same.

She saw a brown girl, just like herself,
take a symphony down from the shelf.
Where limitation is so often placed,
she witnessed the captor's lie erased.

She saw that cellist pluck those strings,
and imagined herself as a thousand things...
the confidence born in this tiny frame,
whose life will never be the same.

Inspired by Marshunda Smith, Cellist, Composer, Conductor
North Shore Juneteenth Association "Hat and Heels" Tea, May 7, 2022

Tell Me Another Bedtime Story

Is this where the sandman picks up each grain,
restoring the beauty,
reducing the pain?
Is this where we fly to Never-Never Land,
like a troop of lost boys with Peter Pan?

All of the mystery of hidden dreams,
nothing now is as it seems.
Tell a sweet tale
that sugars and creams,
with flashes of stardust
and shining moonbeams.

As I lay down to my slumber,
paint a landscape of ochre and umber.
Let there be a hint of romance.
Turn up the quiet...
Love wants to dance.

Tell me a bedtime story please—
of secret gardens and pecan trees,
of babbling brooks and waterfalls,
of gentle breezes that summer calls,
of hidden havens and wondrous spaces,
of astral planes and mystical places.

Let there be a melody,
that sings in four part harmony.
Let it resound in symphony,
then fold into dreamland's reverie.

Tell me a fable
of Arabian nights,

spread on a table
of earthly delights,
free from the label
of anger and fights,
willing and able
to scale higher heights.

Tell me a bedtime story now,
as the baby rocks in the maple bough,
as the blue ox puts his nose to the plow,
and the sweaty farmer wipes his brow,
as each green seedling happily vows,
to yield each fruit the ground allows,
and seven dwarves whistle a happy tune,
and sleeping beauty awakens soon.

Let there be a melody,
that sings in four part harmony.
Let it resound in symphony,
then fold into dreamland's reverie.

This is the time when the sandman whispers—
and seven grooms meet seven sisters.
And the prairie sings an ode to love,
as angels release the turtle-doves.
For now, I lay me down to sleep,
and pray to God my soul to keep.

Color Her Love

Brown is the color of my true love's skin...
the garment that she's most beautiful in.
Impervious to shame and scorn and sin,
brown is the color of my true love's skin.

Red is the color of my true love's blood...
rich as the clay of Georgia's thick mud.
Pure as the rain of a blessing's flood,
red is the color of my true love's blood.

Black is the color of my true love's pride...
worn like a crown and never denied.
Able to sweep blind hate aside,
black is the color of my true love's pride

Green is the color of my true love's seed...
sown in deep soil with never a weed.
Determined to see her progeny freed,
green is the color of my true love's seed.

Lovingly dedicated to my wife, my baby girl's mother, and my partner in life...Teresa J. Carter, always and forever.

Heartbeats

This here little ditty's for the sisters and brothers...
the music of our best days as romantics and young lovers.
It's a Friday night and time to unwind.
The slow jams put us in the mood to grind.
At rent parties, the club, or the hood's rec center,
pay the cover charge before you enter.

Michael Henderson, a boss bass player,
soul singer, artist, back-in-the-dayer...
teamed with Norman Connors and Jean Carne or Phyllis,
Valentine Love or Starship, guaranteed to thrill us.

In the same season, a Delfonics' demise...
so many OG's in shock and surprise.
Poogie Hart's stylishness and lilting falsetto,
La-la means forever and I love you in the ghetto.

R and B royalty sure to be missed,
right there at the spot with the girl you first kissed.
2022, the year we lost them both...
So much soulful history made us take that oath,
to always remember that somebody loves you.
Thank you my brothers for saying this is true.

Dedicated to Michael Henderson and William "Poogie" Hart,
Rest in Melody's Sweet Peace, July 2022

Athene's Riff for Stevie

Perhaps Little Stevie got that thing
from the words of Martin Luther King,
professing love as a need for all
of God's creation, great and small.

So, I'm just breaking in to say,
that love's in need of love today.
Don't let hate and anger bite you.
Let this poet now invite you.

Stevie Wonder may have been blind,
but he had a song for all mankind...
So Athene, I'm here to say,
Love's in need of love today.

Honoring my Sister-friend, the Beantown songstress Athene Wilson,
June 3, 2022

Jazz Jawns

It got into my ears...
way before I could see
what it was,
or understand
why it was,
or even really dig
how it was.
I only knew
that it was
in my ears.

Then it oozed
like hot wax,
down my throbbing chest
and into my pulsing heart.
It made me a slave to the syncopation,
shackled to improvisation...
a rhythm renegade,
a groove gangster,
a jazz junkie.
Dig, dug, done.

I shared Monk's madness.
I craved Miles' blue moods.
I dove into Duke's genius.
I rode Trane's track...
bounced to Dizzy's bop,
and got drunk on Lady Day's *Lover Man* Liqueur,
Sassy's *Speak Low* Sangrias,
and Stray's *Lush Life* Manhattans.

How could a straight-laced brother like me
get drawn into such *Epistrophy*?

How could the rhythm of each new note,
make my blood race like a cigarette boat.
But not at all like a casual fling,
I stuck like glue to the jazz of the thing.
Wed forever to vinyl brides,
mint 33's on Marantz guides...
jazz like tendons attached to my joints,
stretched real taut to the anchor points.

The Birth of the Cool
was my sweet revelation,
an open door
to a whole new sensation...
fused with the funk
in three quarter notation,
the drum and the bass
in cosmic vibration,
echoing forth
in dynamic creation.

It got into my ears...
way before I could see
what it was,
or understand
why it was,
or even really dig
how it was.
I only knew
that it was
in my ears.

Live at the Village Vanguard

Was it the mood of the Bill Evans Trio on Sunday,
or Thad Jones jumpin' with Mel Lewis on Monday?

Where has the jazz met the best of cool jive?
Where are the bees always buzzin' in the hive?

The Trane 'bout to cook the chickens in this yard.
Miles played his heart out at the Village Vanguard.

If you ain't hip, ask someone who knows,
who's on the skins and which bad cat blows.

Eighty-five years and a l'il bit more...
all the great players comin' through that door.

Mingus and Rollins, Monk and McRae,
The MJQ and Anita O'Day,
The Marsalis Nation, Silver and Getz,
Wes Montgomery playin' cool sets,
Dexter Gordon, Roach and Rahsaan,
Cannonball Adderley lit up the barn...
Dizzy Gillespie recorded live,
none of the filler, all of the jive.

The bop, the ballads, the avant garde—
incredibly gorgeous, impossibly hard...

Old Max got shed of beat poems and folk,
He put off the egg whites and served up the yolk.

If you weren't down, you stayed at home.
This was the place for the big dogs to roam.

A thousand recordings, no ersatz, no spam.
This was the spot where the real ones would jam.

Street cred for any whose ears were charred.
You heard it live at the Village Vanguard.

New Jacks and Janes, they heard the call too.
To hang out in Greenwich, and do what they do.
Terri and Geri and Esperanza...
laid out a brand new extravaganza.
Joshua Redmon and Christian McBride,
pushed the limits of standards aside.
Motian, Lovano, and Bill Frisell...
Top-tier trios, alive and well.
Allen Toussaint with the N'awlins groove—
and Terence Blanchard, harmonically smooth.
Roy Hargrove and a boss quintet...
live recordings of more than one set.

Some would call it Cool's Camelot.
Everyone knows that this is the spot.

A Carnegie Hall of untouchable swing...
7th Ave. South got that Big Apple bling.

The giants all come to hit the beat hard...
while the jazzheads lounge, at the Village Vanguard.

--Streams--

"We should all be as water which is lower than all things yet stronger even than the rocks."

Oglala Sioux Proverb

A River Runs Through It

Our valley is a place of legacy...
Colonial towns that stand the test of time,
old graveyards that echo our lost prime,
thoughts that bring a poet to a rhyme—
And a river runs through it.

Our valley is a place of history...
Heroes that fought in all our wars,
pride in service that extend their tours,
courage seeping like sweat through their pores—
and a river runs through it.

Our valley is a place of misery...
Native kindness lost in exploitation,
liberties of some through subjugation,
faith distortions used to build a nation,
hopeful spirits lost at every station—
and a river runs through it.

Our valley is a place of shame.
Treaties were violated.
Tribes were decimated.
Disease was exacerbated.
Environment was devastated.
Greed was celebrated—
and a river runs through it.

Our valley is a place of industry.
Iron was smelted.
Ships were built.
Leather was tanned.
Cloth was dyed.
Rum was distilled.

Glass was blown.
Metal was stamped.
Milk was homogenized
pasteurized and fortified—
and a river runs through it.

Our valley is a place of injury...
White guilt that paralyzes
Black lives trying to matter,
as brown skin is made to scatter...
Homes that only sell to some,
banks don't lend to everyone...
Police don't always serve and protect.
Attitudes breed such disrespect—
and a river runs through it.

Our valley is a place of perjury...
Lies were told as papers passed,
covenants never intended to last,
stolen lands, so much wealth amassed,
rampant corruption, now put on blast.
How did it get so bad, so fast?
And a river runs through it.

Our valley is a place of nativity...
First Americans or slaves in captivity,
abiding gospels of time and space,
every religion and every race,
avenging spirits of fire and ice,
a thousand types of beans and rice—
and a river runs through it.

Our valley is a place of fertility...
Verdant shores by the sandy beaches,
nature grows what the soul beseeches.

Ash and elm and maple preaches,
from the silent spring to the epic speeches—
and a river runs through it.

Our valley is a place of promise...
schools that teach the children with brilliance,
families growing strong with resilience.
Style concedes to the need for substance.
God's design puts the fates in balance.
Community embraced a common will.
Fathers built cities on the tallest hill.
Poems were written that resonate still—
and a river runs through it.

Our valley is a place of revolution...
where the new wars are fought
with philanthropic largesse,
with button-downed lawyers,
and buttoned-up politicos,
with rights of way, injunctive relief,
community forums,
and 10-year Master Plans—
and a river runs through it.

Our valley is a place of revelation...
where acronym associations rebuild,
rebrand, reimagine, and re-engineer,
where volunteers pick and pack and pluck
the refuse from marsh and shore and muck.
Bystanders look and say, "good luck"—
and a river runs through it.

Our valley is a place of vibrancy...
that takes great pride in its energy,
that seeks out moments of synergy,

that wraps its mottos in honesty,
that guards its resources zealously—
and a river runs through it.

Our valley is still a place of denial...
The landed gentry remains on trial,
for sins committed in the church's aisle,
and failure to turn equality's dial,
and actions thought both vain and vile—
and a river runs through it.

Our valley is a place of desecration...
where progress unearths a first civilization,
with legacies stolen to birth a new nation,
with never a notion toward real preservation,
and a headlong rush toward gentrification—
and a river runs through it.

Our valley is a place of rebirth...
where good people meet to set things right,
and the clean-up ensues through the waning light,
and then the party takes over the night,
and the food and music is out of sight—
and a river runs through it.

Inspired by the work of the Mystic River Watershed Association (MyRWA), June 2022

Beach Day?

The Karen and Kevin couple
stands on their carefully manicured lawn
and takes down the plate number
of their Carlos and Carlotta LatinX cousins,
parked in front of their classic New England colonial.

Cousins from the race of man,
who only had a simple plan...
to walk down the hill
and spend a day at the beach.
Joyful niños in gleeful tow,
floaties and coolers, down they go—
out of sight, but not out of mind...

Next step, the 9-1-1 call...
that brings the Police Interceptor
and the local JERR-DAN flatbed.
These people this...
and those people that...
and not in my backyard.

Prerogative rules these situations,
no warnings or tense interrogations.
Meanwhile, Kyle and Kimberly,
the Karen and Kevin kiddos,
fresh off a dip in their in-ground pool...
watch through the bay window and wonder why.
We've got a driveway
and a two-car detached garage.

They wonder,
is this really that big a deal?
Their "cousins" don't come to

stalk, or stain, or steal...
They walk down to the beach,
to swim and have a meal...

But children live what they learn.
At some point,
the persistence of that puritan privilege,
will have them shouting down equity too.

Beloved community?
It's no day at the beach.

River Watch

These Mystic waters have their flow.
Into the Boston Bay they go,
where scullers and kayaks seldom row,
where barges haul and tugboats tow.

A mighty river that takes its name
from a native chieftain of quiet fame,
so many waters did the same,
ironic twists of history's frame.

Sullied by modern man's affairs,
cause and effect, no shores were spared.
Passionate activists raise the cares,
to move the hurt development bares.

Reasoned progress elevates
action that communicates,
respect for our communal places,
retaining Mother Nature's graces.

Who looks to make this bounty fair,
for all who come to gather there?
For all who crave to make this equal,
who looks to write a righteous sequel?

Beyond the bio-diversity,
we're seeking greater equity.
We can't have gleaming waterfront spaces,
without a welcome to black and brown faces.

Who responds when precious green
no longer yields what's pure and clean...
no sanded beachfronts, once pristine,
no sparkling lakesides, crystalline.

Who does triage and mitigation,
when industry brings devastation?
Who gives voice to just frustration,
when all can see the degradation?

Industries that lacked foresight,
commerce created open blight,
that caused the river much distress,
and placed it under real duress.

Invasive plants still choke the stream,
hiding the surface from sunny gleam.
What movement gathers yearly steam,
to realize a hopeful dream?

Here are folks that love the river...
its widest expanse, to its smallest sliver.
Always intent on being a giver,
they cleanse the system like a liver.

All the towns and cities connected,
a living resource must be protected.
So many mistakes have caused it harm,
and stolen from its native charm.

The watershed has life for all.
Winter and Spring, Summer and Fall...
The natural order of all these things,
must face the rising tide change brings.

There's no brass lamp with three great wishes,
to bring back flora, fauna, and fishes.
There's only a band of human power,
sworn to restore sweet nature's flower.

A little fanfare attends this labor.
The invitation goes out to all.
Come and join your Mystic neighbor,
as we answer duty's call.

We'll chart the river's changing path
with engineers; yes there'll be math.
We'll watch environmental clues,
reveal techniques that we can use.

Mystic waters beckon each
to many lessons we can teach,
as eagles soar above the banks,
and avid birders all give thanks.

She needs our help to save the waters,
for all succeeding generations.
For swans and trout and river otters,
we must resist all infestations.

We work to choke off litter's swell.
We gather when we hear the bell.
We work to count the herring schools,
with volunteers and simple tools.

We know the climate is heating up,
and troubling signs may soon erupt.
We raise the anthem of alarm,
to ward off all impending harm.

 Across the span of this great stream,
we've built a strong, dynamic team...
who come to us from far and wide,
to do what others never tried.

Our champions move to aid the scene.
Sometimes they mobilize the green,
that buys the rakes, and booms, and brushes,
that scoop the filth from fronds and rushes.

Our champions lift the banners high,
when others offer cold alibi.

They stay committed to the cause,
when legislators sit and pause.

At the river's edge today,
we gather again to celebrate,
so much progress along the way,
five decades to enumerate.

Champions are in the room,
to echo and to amplify...
the mission of our heart's desire,
to never let the river die.

Champions offer new perspectives,
partnerships and collaborations...
as we seek to meet objectives,
for these Mystic preservations.

Champions mind the river's bends,
meanderings and undulations.
The Mystic needs these loyal friends,
and all their noble motivations.

Beyond each drop of sweet spring rain,
let this flood each heart and brain.
In case your efforts may have missed them,
embrace all in the ecosystem.

This river poet's single goal,
to let you know it has a soul,
with love for all and hate for none,
please help the Mystic River run.

I've used up every clever pun.
Please help the mighty Mystic run.

Inspired by the work of the Mystic River Watershed Association (MyRWA), Annual
Champion's Breakfast, June 2023

Pandemic's Labyrinth

The maze of a malignant truth,
   caught in a pandemic telephone booth...
we have few havens of true resistance,
   no outgoing calls, no directory assistance,
   no change in our pockets...
   and no one will accept the charges.

There were all these appealing entrances
   that ended as appalling exits.
The genesis of a terrible disease,
   the exodus of life as we once knew it.
The numbers are beyond our comprehension.
Our disbelief in total suspension,
   such an activation of abject fear,
a depression we can't seem to put in the rear.

It's not the road less traveled.
It's a labyrinth of hoses, tubes,
   aspirators and heartbreak,
   heaving chests,
   and loneliness,
   collisions, hope against hope,
   somber declarations,
   and divided nations.

So many doors that we seem content to bar...
   no bridges of mercy to cross, so far.
All six degrees of separation,
   a seventh sign of human damnation,
   feelings abound of eternal perdition,
   a pivotal break in the human condition.
Half of the country in open sedition,
   and now we're fighting a war of attrition.

We can breathe right here
and ponder this,
no hasty embrace,
no saccharin kiss.
We can meditate upon a rock,
no key to open this Covid lock,
with current to cause a viral shock,
new toxic strains on every block.

The minotaur was once
imprisoned in a maze like this.
Designed in myth by cunning Daedalus...
dispatched in myth by hero Theseus.

But current monsters blocked by hedge and thorn,
match the terror of such a beast reborn...
plunging us headlong toward doubt and fear.
That question posed again,
"What road leads out of here?"

And if we manage to escape,
what mutations force our mouths agape?
What pestilence may enter unabated,
and become new death that penetrated?
If we only move to build new walls,
the scourge will quickly move through all our halls.
And yet the wisdom to be won,
seems to be the thing from which we run.

It's not the road less traveled.
It's a labyrinth of inoculations,
masks and avoidance,
of separations,
heavy sighs,
and isolation,
of commitments, hope against hope,
of somber declarations...
and divided nations.

Lessons from the Corona's Edge

I asked my facebook friends what they learned in 2021.

They told me many things...
wise things,
wistful things,
wild things,
wonderful things,
woeful things,
wayward things,
wrathful things,
worthy things.

They said:

"I learned that after losing my parent, I can still move forward,
to serve God with a smile and a song in my heart."

"When I put my mind to something, I can make things happen..."

"that I have more patience than I thought I had."

"I learned that God exists not only in the miraculous and wonderful
spaces; He also exists in the terrifying and "tore up, from the floor up"
places. He will meet you wherever you are!"

"...Ooowee...could write a book...and I did...2 in fact...in a
nutshell: This is the day of trouble, but it is also the day of the Lord...
take comfort in that & rejoice & be glad in Him."

"I learned the true meaning of having a relationship with Him."

"that I can have more peace when I distance myself from toxicity and
ignorance."

"that what you really want, and what you really need...may reside in two totally different realities."

"Two things I learned is that God is a good, good Father and how to partner up with the Holy Spirit.'

"I learned to wait on him. He will restore and renew your soul. I am a true believer in the power of prayer"

"In Him I live, move, and have my being. God is truly a way maker."

"The same sun shines on everyone."

"I learned resiliency."

"I learned the more I know the more there is to learn...good to be a lifelong learner."

"That throughout this pandemic, God's plan for my life has been sustaining and ever-evolving."

"I sing songs about surrendering my all to Jesus, but I learned that I'm actually doing it."

"I learned that religion can be a fickle thing, but God is constant all the time."

"I learned that the same folks who can love their own children without limits, can hate yours without rhyme, or reason, or shame."

"That the virus doesn't care about your politics, but some folks believe their personal freedoms cancel out your right to health and well-being."

"that prejudice comes in every color of the rainbow, that love comes in every color of the rainbow, that lies come in every color of the rainbow."

"I learned that everybody wants to go to heaven, but nobody really wants to die."

"What I cherish the most, money could never buy."

I asked them what they learned in 2021.

They told me many things...
wise things,
wistful things,
wild things,
wonderful things,
woeful things,
wayward things,
wrathful things,
worthy things.

Coronavirus Blues: A Pandemic Poem

No toilet paper at the store,
what did I even go shopping for?

This mask is giving my face a rash.
I just want to throw it in the trash.

Latex gloves, they make me scratch.
So now I wear an allergy patch.

Hand sanitizer's chafing my skin...
sad to reflect on the shape we're in.

I'm washing my hands like Lady MacBeth.
I can't stand to hear of another friend's death.

My birthday party happened on Zoom.
No one else was in the room.

The cars paraded on down my street...
with balloons, but somehow, incomplete.

My kids missed prom and graduation.
Look what this thing has done to our nation.

How do we keep from freaking out?
Whose advice are we seeking out?
All of our patience is leaking out,
of this living we're barely eking out.

Red state rogues won't stay in their lane,
going to rallies and spreading the strain.

Can't see Gramps in the nursing home...
hoping and praying he's keeping Shalom.

YaYa says it's Greek to me.
How can I love on my family?

What if my Stavros doesn't come back,
victimized by this viral attack?

Fatality toll is rising each day.
Why can't our leaders find the right way?

The virus is pushing us over the edge...
carving us up with a razor-sharp wedge,
chasing us onto a dangerous ledge.
Can't we just chill? Can't we just veg'?

These are the days that try men's souls.
They're raking us parents over the coals.

They'll use the tablet to play Fortnight...
but not to keep their math skills tight.

So tired of having kids in my face...
don't they have to go someplace?

I want to get dressed and just go to work.
When did this teen become such a jerk?

Who came up with this hybrid model?
That's the one I just need to throttle.

It's traumatizing to us poor teachers...
like Red Sox fans in the Yankee bleachers.

I feel so bad for the local shops...
the cafes, and all the mom and pops,
for the EMTs, the nurses, and cops.
Will they be okay when this madness stops?
Will we find some bottoms to go with our tops,
when the last Zoom classroom finally drops?

Betrothals can't have a proper wedding...
and churches face some really tough sledding.

Live-streamed preaching and virtual Jesus,
somehow doesn't totally please us.

I just can't seem to shake these blues.
Is there some potion I can use?

Doctors say to stay at home.
Time to finish this Covid poem.

Social distance gets magnified,
as feuding families choose a side.

Political football gets tossed around,
not an ounce of civility found.

What the left wants, the right won't give.
Meanwhile, sick people struggle to live.

This mask is giving my face a rash.
I just want to throw it in the trash.

Latex gloves, they make me scratch.
So now I wear an allergy patch.

I've got those coronavirus blues...
My mind I think I'm going to lose.

Sad to reflect on the shape we're in...
pray that the virus doesn't win.

Breaking Glass

My former interns now have crow's feet
and growing families of their own.
They're lawyers, accountants, judges,
engineers, bankers, and corporate officers.
Some are in C-suites, looking down
at glass floors.

They still email me, or post small social media tributes
to my place in their success stories,
to the inroads I helped them make,
to the wisdom I shared,
the gentle steering I provided...
and the grief I helped them avoid.

Pride is so often exaggerated and misplaced...
and to mimic the bard,
it fairly always goeth before a fall.
Yet I will risk the potential mishap,
to dote on my spiritual children,
for through misted eyes, I must genuflect...

They have made me a proud father.

Honoring my time at INROADS, Inc., 1998-2009

The Kids Are Alright

Don't be too hard on them…
saying that youth is wasted on the young,
lamenting their impetuousness and their impertinence.
You must not remember how it once was,
how you once were,
what you had to learn,
and what you had to unlearn,
in order to be the you
you've become.

Don't be too quick to judge.
They are coming into their own.
They are getting the revelation,
having the epiphany,
seeing the forest for the trees.
You weren't always so perfect,
so wise in your ways,
so prudent in your decisions,
so fair-minded,
so reasonable,
so level-headed.

Don't revise your past mistakes
out of your current history.
They inform the cut of your character.
Let them grow into their big boy pants,
and their big girl pants,
and their non-binary pants,
and their "I'll let you know when I know pants."
Let them form their own allegiances
and declare their own agency,
and not carry the water
of your conflicts and battlefields.

Let them be diverse.
Let them be non-racist
and non-violent.
Let them be vegan and vegetarian.
Let them be safely mischievous.
Let them be environmentally-conscious.
Let them be politically astute
and boldly outspoken,
and just plain out.
Let them be financially literate.
Let them be tolerant.
Let them be allies.
Let them be poetic and romantic
and funny (ha-ha)...
Let them be saved by faith through God.
Let them be youthfully exuberant
and legitimately curious.

Just let them be.

And remember...
the kids are alright.

Just let them be...

The kids are alright.

Sand

Once a man or woman,
but twice a baby too...
this seems the natural way of things.
And it couldn't be more true.

Although you've lived a century,
and weathered every storm,
I change your diaper daily.
That's once again the norm.

Your speech is urgent gibberish,
I've learned to understand.
You cry out and you flail your arms,
in making each demand.

I don't hold this against you,
though my patience may run thin.
This surreal role reversal,
is just the stage we're in.

Your memory has now slipped away.
You sometimes cannot tell,
that I'm that blessed infant,
you claimed from heaven fell.

So now this child you treasured
and treated with such care,
manages your every need,
each grey and crinkled hair.

A dozen medications,
they've prescribed for your condition...
Religiously I push them down,
to sponsor your remission.

You curse me like a sailor,
when you're angry or in pain.
Still you are a cherished gift.
I try not to complain.

And to my sons and daughters,
I make this humble plea:
Do not shed my wrinkled hide,
when old age gets to me.

Do not think me useless,
and place me in a home,
where underpaid, uncaring hosts,
just leave me alone.

Let me move toward heaven,
from a safe, familiar place.
Let me have my dignity,
and a measure of God's grace.

Once a man or woman,
for the second time a child...
this rebirth isn't pretty,
and the symptoms are not mild.

The little lamb you once led
into pastures full and green,
has now become your shepherd,
toward fields peaceful and serene.

I've written down the history
for our young ones to remember...
each amazing year you've lived,
January to December.

I cherish even the menial task...
To serve you is my choice.

Although you'd never think to ask,
the plague has claimed your voice.

This spectrum that they speak of,
is such a bitter pill,
the brightest of His children
regressed in thought and skill.

I watch you seep away like sand,
in an hourglass once so clear.
And yet each grain remaining,
assures that I'll be here

Each precious grain remaining...
assures that I'll be here.

The New Temple

The molded steel, red clay brick, and tempered glass
yields now to curious children in soft chairs, after class,
settling in to the wi-fi hub, books, and the next homework task,
into the lap of wonder they sit and bask.

We can't be a greater city without this scene.
We can't alter a culture, that's sometimes harsh and mean.
We can't help them to crave the peaceful and serene.
We can't show them pastures, literate, sweet and green.

The ramps now flank the steps to make a way,
for those that fairly skipped, back in their day.
Now audiobooks and dvds accrue,
inviting these elders in to join the queue.
The generations all must have their say.
All these voices have a part to play,
each anticipating this auspicious day.

Once upon a time in Medford's West,
a tiny branch of wisdom was our nest.
Such traditions may not now survive...
but what they represent is still alive.

That little room at the fire station,
fueled this poet's imagination.
Now my words can help us celebrate
what a grand new space may now create.

Mrs. Christ and Sister Lynne,
helped to mold the shape I'm in.
Librarians opened this special gift,
that gives our hearts and minds uplift.

No horned-rimmed glasses now to bid us hush...
so many good things to treasure and to touch,

so many discoveries that make us all a-gush,
so many new riches that make us fairly blush.
The mommies will come with babies in tow.
The story-tellers will weave as they sew,
characters lively with color and sound…
and new traditions surely will be found.

Spacious rooms, airy and filled with light,
have beckoned new friends to an open invite.
Places we'll meet and collaborate,
perhaps to dispel suspicion and hate.
We will make this a home for spirit and art,
with a unified vision, right from the start.

The plans did call for some gleam and glamour.
But not to distract, to show off, or enamor.
This is the face of our brave new world.
Here is a space where our banner's unfurled.

A proud son's legacy lends the name,
Bloomberg largesse, now wraps the frame.
Our people fairly rush to crowd the space,
a look of wonder framing every face.
Now the wee ones amplify the glow,
while the old ones wisely take is slow.
Where are you going, so cheerful and merry?
To our wonderful new, public library.

The molded steel, red clay brick, and tempered glass,
yield now to the sound of wisdom growing inside,
crossing those borders which sometime divide,
so common concern may freely reside,
and the beacon of learning is multiplied.
We can be a great city because of this scene.
We can alter a culture that's sometimes harsh and mean.
We can each go to places we've not ever been.

A temple of sorts, where eons of wisdom tell
the stories of this warm and human shell,
the legends of our past who rose and fell,
the dreams plucked from our wishing well.
A temple of sorts, where fables meet with truth,
where testimony finds confession's booth,
where theories offer bright and shining proof
of how the ancients never left their youth.

A proud son's legacy lends the name,
a Bloomberg gift, now wraps this modern frame.
Our people fairly rush to crowd the space,
a look of wonder framing every face.
Now the wee ones amplify the glow,
while the old ones wisely take is slow.

Where are you going, so cheerful and merry?
To our wonderful new, public library.

Commissioned for the dedication of the new
Charlotte and William Bloomberg Medford Public Library,
Medford, MA
December, 2021

--Motion--

"Let your nature be known and proclaimed."

Huron Proverb

The Art of Living

Follow the landscape into the field,
and see what colors the earth might yield,
tones of umber and ochre hue,
viridian green and cobalt blue.

Flow with the brook to rivers and sea.
Paint the wave-tossed mystery.
Sculpt the rock with a hammer and spike.
Take a picture and post for a like.

The art of living is imitation.
It spurs the hand to bright creation.
In the studio loft or imagination,
living with art is a revelation.

The writer puts a pen to page,
or opens a screen to the digital age.
Though yet it's an uncanny thing,
that God made a poet and bid him sing.

The potter throws with heart and zeal.
The clay finds form on his spinning wheel.
The firing process shows the proof,
that art has found a special truth.

And then the play commands the stage.
The playwright frees a wish from its cage.
The fates and tides have opened doors,
for actors to strut on theater floors.

Trumpet and strings and drums resound.
You hear the symphony all around.
And all who witness soon rejoice,
at the majesty of the human voice.

These gifts bestowed by a loving God,
the realms through which the arts have trod,
fragrant seeds from a verdant pod...
always in truth, never by fraud...
creating pathways to the soul,
beyond the reach of mind control.

AI can't replace creative zeal...
though sentience, it rushes in to steal.
The natural has its own unique appeal...
eschews the fake, and uplifts the real.

So let the poets have their say,
as sunrise beckons each new day.

Circumspection

I have not yet learned to walk rightly among men at all times.
Haughtiness connects me to indignation at the smallest slights.
I expect to be treated fairly in all transactions, when in truth,
I have played the cheat on more than a few occasions.

I have called the name of God in vain all too frequently.
My faith can be challenged by the tiniest of tests.
I bristle at authority and the most righteous of rebukes...
delivered by good souls of great wisdom.

Though I have love for all men, I truly like but a few.
My patience can be painfully thin and far too easily tried.
While I have mastered the fragrant sweetness of flowery words,
I am just as likely to aim the barbs of an acid tongue at a hapless victim.

This moment's lucid musings are no source of pride.
I have so much to apologize for,
so many recriminations,
so much forgiveness to crave.

And yet, a good, good Father
has cast my sin and indiscretion into a boundless sea
of eternal forgetfulness.
I may yet learn to walk rightly among men, circumspectly,
and in due season.

Runnin' My Race

You tryin' to get me to disavow critical race theory.
It's something you all find Stephen King scary.
You're sick of this push for greater inclusion;
so you sow the seeds of racial confusion.
You want my blackness to quietly fade,
into the lies and denial you made.
You tryin' to get me to be as unconscious,
of the righteous aspects of myself as you are.
You want me to keep assimilating,
as all around me, you keep hating.
You want me to shrink into a shell,
while you make my life a living hell.

Don't even think about it...

I'm gonna love me, see.
I'm gonna love my negritude...
and my attitude...
and my aptitude.
I'm gonna love my blackness in all of its diversity.
I'm gonna praise my roots in all of their complexity.
I'm gonna swim in the flow of the Nile,
and the Congo,
and the Ganges,
and the Amazon,
and the Yangtze,
and the Mississippi...
that's flowin' in me.

I'm gonna thrive on fruit of the spirit,
and the tripartite divinity
that connects me to the universality
of the echoes of my ancestry.
I'm gonna wrap my mind around the duality

of my original state of captivity,
and my current quest for community.
I'm gonna revel in my multifarious vicissitudes,
my blissfully soulful interludes,
and my "don't mess with me today" funky moods.

You want me to throttle down
my celebration of cultural resplendency,
while you ratchet up acceptance
of your notions of white supremacy.
You want to make America great again,
one less brown-skinned boy at a time,
four less little black girls at a time,
hundreds fewer immigrant children at a time,
thousands fewer dreamers at a time,
millions fewer registered voters at a time.
Right now...today...
not tomorrow...
not next week...next month...or next year!

But just so you know me...
and where I'm coming from, see...
Black Lives Matter and we won't be put to scatter.
Despite the hate crimes and the daily killings,
the vitriol and the blood that keeps spilling.
We are gonna love ourselves.
We're gonna embrace our allies
and denounce our traitors.
We're gonna tell our own stories
and not get silenced by the haters.
We're gonna rally in solidarity
from every single polarity.
We're gonna break the schism
of generational racism.
We're gonna look through a prism
of sacred humanism.

God is on the side of His people.
He's going to rightly divide His word,
and separate the called out ones
into His grace and favor.

You want to bend this precious faith
to your political caprice.
You want to study more war,
instead of spreading love and peace.
It's time to look to the hills
from whence comes our strength,
and then look to extend the span
of the rainbow's length.

You want God to approve your corrupted version
of His word, His way, and His will...
a version that allows you to destroy,
to steal, and to kill.
You want to evangelize a secret genocide.
You want to disciple generational xenophobia.
You want to weaponize pulpits of rage and exclusion.
You want to build walls around perverted faith statements
and let snake oil be your living water.
You want to count it all joy,
that you can kill a black boy.
You want us to panic and run,
when you raise another gun.
You want us to cower and shrink,
instead of strategize and think.

Better check yourself, before you wreck yourself.

Now comes the sunrise hour,
when we'll recognize a new Black power.
Now comes a greater time,
when we'll be lifting as we climb.
See us waking from the silence,

as we fight against this violence.
See us gather with our friends,
as we march 'til hatred ends.
See the allies all assemble,
as we make our demons tremble.

I'm runnin' my race...
Up my sleeve I've got an ace,
to remove that ugly face.
And though you try to chase
with your tasers, guns, and mace,
then set me up to catch a case,
to make prisons my home base,
or vanish with no trace...
I won't slow my pace.

I'm runnin' my race...
as I move beyond this space.
as I speed to find my place
where I'm all about this ace,
no hint of fear upon my face,
where I gladly will embrace
my great God's amazing grace.

So check yourself...
You 'bout to wreck yourself.

We here see.
Black folk, brown folk, tan folk...
folk who look like me...
To all the haters and separators,
here is what I be...

I'm gonna love me, see.
I'm gonna love my negritude...
and my attitude...
and my aptitude.

I'm gonna love my blackness in all of its diversity.
I'm gonna praise my roots in all of their complexity.
I'm gonna swim in the flow of the Nile,
and the Congo,
and the Ganges,
and the Amazon,
and the Yangtze,
and the Mississippi...
that's flowing in' me.

I'm gonna see my finish line,
and it's Godly in design.
It's not a people in decline.
It's not awash in sin or crime.
It's sweet like Champagne wine...
strong as Samson in his prime,
"a brilliant sun," on His green vine,
a truth that's more than simply mine.
I can share and that's just fine...
It's a story most sublime,
shared in just a nick of time.
as I end this final rhyme.

Die Empty

I can't understand a lot of it…
how quickly need morphs into want,
and the necessary disappears
down an avenue of desire.

Baubles and trinkets break our hold
on the truth of hopes and dreams,
becoming bookmarks to happiness
in libraries of gold and gaudiness.

How much is enough?
How many is too many?
Where will it all end?

I've watched the fortunes of my familiars
turn into footnotes of flirtation and epitaph.
They could never get beyond acquisition and avarice.
They could never put aside the piles, and the closets,
and the cases, and the safes,
and the bags, boxes, bows and ribbons…
Stuff is a sad compensation for real love,
and legitimacy, and loyalty.

Can one head be home to a hundred hats…
one wrist to a hundred watches,
one heel to a hundred horseshoes,
one heart to a hundred harbors,
one hip to a hundred holsters,
one silhouette to a hundred suits?

Legacy isn't just a ledger line and a Lamborghini.
Destiny walks out its path resolutely.
It doesn't drag and drift and draft
on asphalt freeways.

Am I brave enough to leave it all behind...
to not be tied to the trappings,
to not be bought by the brag, and the bling, and the banknotes?
Can I find a good and holy space?
Can I tithe into this worthy place?
Can I give toward sweet, redemptive grace?
Can I seek only God's true face?

One fifty thousand dollar bottle of Domaine de la Romanee
in a temperature-controlled francophone stacked stone cellar...
stocked full of vineyard nobility,
what does it really mean to me?
It will never bless my community.

Multimillion dollar yachts will not be
the sovereigns of the seas forever.
The ocean's floor is paved with the rusted hulls of hubris,
the lost treasures of hedonism,
and the toxic heaps of human hoarding.

Waves crash over the shores of sinful gluttony,
and a thousand sirens beckon
souls of shameful avarice to sail closer.
How many more will heed the lilting, but lurid song?
How many more will be dragged and drowned
in their quest for too much,
too many,
and never enough?

How many souls have you neglected,
attending to all the things you've collected...
cataloging and data entry,
watching like a Spartan sentry?
How many embraces have you dismissed
beloved cheeks that were not kissed,
needy saints that just got dissed,
charities just crossed off your list?

Crypto-currency...sounds like dead money
trying to achieve an afterlife,
on shadowy rivers of NFTs,
and Bitcoin for the ferryman.
Ugly houses flipped on countless corners
to feed D-I-N-K appetites for suburban shorelines,
with city amenities, bohemian breakfast nooks,
and hipster appeal.

The prophet said "Die empty!"
Eternity cares not for
the troublesome,
and the tainted,
and the tarnished.
It will all fail and fade away
in due season..

The word of faith says,
it is more blessed to give than to receive.

The word of faith says it is more difficult for a camel
to pass through the eye of a needle,
than for a rich man to enter
the kingdom of heaven.

The word of faith says that ashes and dust
will have dominion,
in due season.

The prophet said "Die empty!"
Heaven holds slim desserts
for the moguls,
and the maniacal,
and the made of money.
It will all fail and fade away
in due season

Die empty...

Find a good and holy space.
Tithe into that worthy place.
Give toward sweet, redemptive grace.
Seek ye only God's true face.

Survivor's Guilt

It gets to me sometimes...
As Marvin Gaye, sang back in the day,
"Makes me wanna holler,
throw up both my hands."

Lord God, you brought home
Nana Jean, Pap, and Baby Boy...
Sweat the oil of your countenance
upon their malignancies,
and canceled the debt
of suffering in their bodies.

Yet I'm still out here on your Word...
missing them desperately, every day,
and wondering...
what is left for me to do?

Cancer came to my doorstep too...
knocked me for a loop.
It messed with my manhood
and made me feel
weaker than,
less than,
unequal to.

The same monster that
waited in the shadows,
and infiltrated their bodies
as a fatal foreign host,
came for me too.
But mercy said "no".

So this restlessness in my spirit
rustles, and rumbles, and rages.

It convicts me sometimes...
questions my raison d'etre,
and moves me to a dark place,
where uncertainty and unworthiness
hold court.

Yet I'm still out here on your Word...
trying hard not to curse my providence,
and wondering...
what is left for me to do?

Through You, I survived.
Jehovah Rapha prayers went up
from everyone in my village,
even though I couldn't be transparent enough,
to tell them exactly what to pray for.
You knew and you graciously accepted
every petition.

You still have work for me to do.
You haven't finished with me yet.
I'm still under construction.
What in the world are you building?

The weight of this survivor's guilt...
will it erode my firm foundation?
Am I the house that was built on sand
and washed away.
Like my Brother Jesus,
am I the stone the builder rejected?

Do I believe?
Does Your word confirm, or condemn?
This is the path, walk ye in it.
The steps of a righteous man are ordered.
God is no respecter of persons.
But to each one of us grace has been given,
as Christ apportioned it.

So, I keep on doing and living,
praying and serving,
watching and giving.
Will it ever be enough?

Are Nana Jean, and Pap, and Baby Boy,
paying attention,
from that expansive heavenly perch?
Can they see the
weaker than,
less than,
and unequal to?
Do they miss me,
desperately and every day?

This survivor's guilt...
it gets to me sometimes.
As Marvin Gaye, sang back in the day,
"Makes me wanna holler,
throw up both my hands."

Who Knew?

People can say all sorts of things, after the fact.
They can make a million pronouncements about
your becoming,
and your arrival,
your accolades,
and accomplishments.
But nobody really knew.
When you were be-bopping and bunny-hopping
in the parks and playgrounds,
ball fields and rec centers,
in your beloved Roxbury...
nobody really knew.
That's just how it goes.

I mean really...

Who knew about
six rings, a Dream Team,
his Airness,
the footwear empire,
fat cigars,
and GOAT status,
when Michael
was just another kid
with a basketball jones?
Carolina blue may have
given a clue;
but let's be real,
nobody truly knew.

When Viola
was struggling to stay alive,
sleeping in her hoopdi,

and just trying to survive...
who the heck would have prophesied
that the Oscar statue would someday reside
on her mantelpiece?
She wasn't on
anyone's short list.
She wasn't Ebony.
or Essence or People,
or hallelujah--Vogue...
back then.

And Bloomberg was just a nerdy Jewish kid from Medford.
Did anyone see that ascension?
Did they see the empires in contention?
Perhaps his business dealings,
bring up all kinds of feelings;
but classmates can recall
he wasn't the mogul type at all.
Powerful news networks,
with billions of dollars in Wall Street perks,
and not the office in his home City Hall...
he went to the Apple
and made those giants fall.
Mayor Bloomberg...
That's not even what folks were trying to say
to little Mikey, back in the day.

I could go on with the global,
but home is for the locals.
And after all, who knew
about our great hero...
about Just Plain Joe?

Who predicted that he'd be a scribe,
fifty years of by-lines and a sporting vibe?
Who among his Herald chums

would equate his rise with Roxbury slums?
Celtics, Bruins, Sox and Pats,
he'd report the home team's trophy hats.
He wrote about the balls and strikes,
before the days of facebook likes.
From Russell and Cousy,
to Tom Terrific,
he was well-informed
and highly specific.
From Bobby Orr to Bergeron,
the ones with brains and the ones with brawn,
the veterans and all the rookies,
before Draft Kings replaced the bookies.

He saw each team hold up the gold.
He made their sagas big and bold.
On 'BZ and on 38,
the news from Joe was never late.

Yet in his heart were new horizons,
ones that meant no compromising.
To social justice and equity,
his pen would turn effectively.
For Christian faith and children's rights,
he'd be right there on special nights.
Always around for loving friends,
he'd be there, where the sidewalk ends.

Speaking the truth in churches and schools,
connecting people, explaining the rules...
athletes, kids, and men of God,
his testimony, a chastening rod.

This concert, his annual labor of love,
his voice and the choir, fit like a glove...
an anchor for these jubilant songs,
extending grace where grace belongs.

A giving soul and heart so true,
this loving tribute is for you.
The poem reports that honor's due,
to a Roxbury kid that changed the view,
a Somerville Sunday we look forward to,
with a guy named Joe Fitzgerald.

Who knew?

Celebrating my Friend and Brother in Christ, Joe Fitzgerald
October, 2022

Six of One, Half-Dozen of the Other

Six brothers met on the Astral Plane...
awaiting God's blessing, fearing God's bane.

Six brothers gave a good confession.
Six brothers missed their intercession.

One brother said he had fed the poor.
One brother said he had shut the damn door.

One brother said he had healed the sick.
One brother said he'd been clever and slick.

One brother said he prayed for the broken.
One brother said "man, you must be jokin.'"

One brother said he fought for justice.
One brother said can't nobody trust us.

One brother said he preached God's word.
One brother said he just followed the herd.

One brother said he told the whole truth.
One brother said he mixed gin with vermouth.

Six brothers left for that next higher plane...
no war, no sickness, and no more pain.

Six brothers left for the depths of hell...
They're still in the fire, as best we can tell.

Church Folk (Haiku Chorus)

Sisters will bring it.
Some will over-sing it.
That's the gospel truth.

Preacher's gettin' paid.
In a five-star room he stayed.
The Word flies first class.

His Caddie, played out.
Said that The Lord told him so.
Buy me a new Benz'...

Kids cut up today.
Elder Sue on vacation.
She ain't havin' it!

Seventh Day

Sometimes doing nothing speaks to the spirit too.
Thus, lazy is also a language.
Indolence is not always lacking effort,
and ennui has its place.
Let the bodies in motion stay in motion.
Bodies at rest are cool too.
I'm not mad at the joggers,
and the power walkers,
and the gym rats,
and the workout mavens.
I'm not sucking my teeth at the early risers
and the "energizer bunnies"
that keep on going and going and going...
God bless the rushing waters,
and the rolling hills,
and the racing blood.
May He also send a quieter grace
to the babbling brook,
and the meandering meadow,
and the silent spring.
Reclined is not declined,
any more than resting is protesting,
any more than chilling means unwilling,
any more than entropy means atrophy.
Relaxing is biblical too.
The Lord rested on the Seventh day...
and Mary tarried at the feet of Jesus,
much to the chagrin of Martha,
but perfectly okay with the Master.
Sometimes doing nothing
speaks to the spirit too.

Evangelical Fraud

If you have decided that compassion and kindness and love and basic humanity have to take a back seat to your desire to be better than your darker-skinned neighbor and supremely white in every aspect, please understand that there is a cost for feeling this way. God is not looking at you as a favorite child right now. He sees how diminished you are in the fruits of the spirit and He is saddened and angry. He didn't create you to be this way. You have abandoned the hope of His glory for your own gain, your own greed, your own jealousies and insecurities, and your own pride. Any claim you want to make to Christian spirituality is built on a horrible lie. Doesn't matter whether you're the preacher at a 5000 seat church, or the truck driver from Mobile, Alabama. You can't walk in the wake of hate, for any man, or any woman, or any child--simply because of the color of their skin--and still claim the brotherhood of Christ as your legacy.

Whatever rationalization you have heard, embraced, or created to justify this hate is a lie from the pit of hell. "God is not a man, that he should lie; neither the son of man, that he should repent..." (Numbers 23:19) You're playing a dangerous game with eternity. I believe that unbridled hate and unchecked vanity will be the chief causes of eternal perdition in the last days. Heaven has no room for it, just as God has no tolerance for those who would mock His commandment to love one another, even as Christ has loved us. When the rapture comes, soon and very soon, those who blindly hate, will not be gathered up with Jesus Christ. They will rather inherit the whirlwind and be cast into the proverbial sea of fire... certainly not a hope of mine, rather a simple truth of the Gospels.

White supremacy and Christian evangelism are as far apart from one another as the North Pole is from the South. That kind of vengeful pride and violent intent cannot live peaceably, quietly or out loud, in the body of Christ. I don't know what kind of pastors have the temerity and gall to stand behind a sacred desk and suggest, imply, exegete, or "hermeneut" otherwise. Racist hatred is sin...and God is no respecter of titles or false doctrine. The prophets of a white identity lifestyle and other exclusionary tropes will be struck down in due season. This is an inevitable consequence of preaching against God's basic commandment to love, and love unconditionally.

If you want to make the argument that "all lives matter", that's fine. Just understand that if you make that pronouncement, while harboring an irrational fear and loathing of Black men, you've lied. If you make that global pronouncement, while teaching your children that the white man is inherently more intelligent, more god-like, more worthy, and more "American" than any person of color, particularly Black people, you've lied. If you go to church every Sunday and recite the "Lord's Prayer", while in your heart knowing that you wish that Black people would "go back where they came from" or be killed off by the COVID-19 storm, you've lied.

Now white folks lie to Black folks every day. I'm not naive, the last fifty years don't change the first 350. In every institutional area, from policing and criminal justice, to employment and educational access...you lie to us. You lie about banking and finance. You lie about free speech and gun rights. You lie about housing and food security. You lie about environmental atrocity and public health. The lie is fundamental to the process of dominating other people and stealing what doesn't belong to you. We get it. We fight it every day of our lives...but we get it.

Here is the lie we don't get. We don't get you lying to God the Father, God the Son, and God the Holy Spirit about being part of the Body of Christ. You can't be serious. You're killing us in the streets, in our cars, in our own homes on a daily basis for the sole reason of our blackness. You're having rallies in god-forsaken haunts and hollows, extolling the superior virtues of your white identity and making pacts to eliminate us from the American landscape by violent means...Heck, you're burning crosses to symbolize your hatred. I can't find any of this in my Bible...and neither can you. On the other hand, you're all about the Beatitudes, Ecclesiastes, and the poetry of the Psalms. Until you all bought red MAGA caps, you were often seen with John 3:16 caps at sporting events and the gun club.

Evangelical Fraud is taking place in this country on a massive scale. It's in many ways akin to the religious fraud that took place in Germany in the ramp up to the Third Reich and Hitler's annihilation of the Jews across Europe. You see, most scholars believe that if the 60 million "Christians" in Germany had taken an immediate stand against the politics and propaganda of Hitler and his Nazi minions, the Holocaust might never have happened. But right now, a significant and growing cadre of evangelical leaders in the Deep South and in the American heartland have cast their lots with the rightfully deposed president and his base of the extreme white right. Their congregations are walking lock-step with those leaders and denying basic biblical principles all over the righteousness roadmap. Agape love is off the list. Thou shalt not lie is off the list. Thou shalt not kill is off the list. Thou shalt not covet is off the list. Taking the name of the Lord in vain is off the list. Making idols and worshipping graven images is off the list.

Oh, there's lots more...but perhaps we should also take a look at what's on the list.

Killing unarmed black men, women and children is on the list. Condoning 940 hate groups (according to the Southern Poverty Law Center) is on the list. An unprecedented escalation in the personal ownership of militaristic weapons is on the list. Rationalizing domestic terrorism is on the list. Bumping up the power of the police state is on the list. Criminalizing immigration and punishing the children of asylum seekers and American dreamers is on the list. Railing against all stripes of diversity, from gender to race to economic status, is on the list. Prohibiting, by legal and illegal means, the right of marginalized people to vote freely and without apprehension is on the list. And yes, all but idolizing a former president whose lack of leadership, personal character, and public deportment are far and away the worst in American history, is clearly on the list.

Lastly, as a man of God, I detest taking other "avowed" men and women of God to task. I truly do. The pit in my stomach deepens with every word I write. But I remain that Habakkuk 2:2-3 scribe. My task is as my talent has been given—to 2 "Write down the revelation and make it plain on tablets so that a herald may run with it. 3 For the revelation awaits an appointed time; it speaks of the end and will not prove false. Though it linger, wait for it; it will certainly come and will not delay."

Jackleg to Jingoist, Southern Baptist, COGIC, or Catholic... evangelical fraud is not of God. There's a bed of lies in the Body of Christ that will soon move God to justice. Perhaps you won't be prosecuted, but you sure enough will be persecuted. God is not looking at you as a favorite child right now. He sees how diminished you are in the fruits of the spirit and He is saddened and angry. He didn't create you to be this way.

You better get ready. Judgment day is coming and all those guns and ammo you're stockpiling aren't going to protect you. The backwoods bivouacs and "good old boys" aren't going to protect you. The "panic-rooms" and gated communities aren't going to protect you. The stocks, and bonds, and trust funds, and annuities, and gold, and diamonds, and bit-coin, and fine art, and academic degrees, and Lamborghinis, and Cape Cod cottages, and Coral Gables condos, and Myrtle Beach bungalows, and Aspen chalets, and San Clemente cul-de-sacs aren't going to protect you. And no, coronavirus vaccinations aren't going to protect you either.

God don't like ugly.

That's my story and I'm sticking to it.

The Refreshing

We keep it fresh my friends.
Not because the first thing
wasn't a good thing,
a timely thing,
an honorable thing,
even a historic thing...

But because the next thing matters too.
It extends equity.
It doubles down on diversity.
It invests in inclusion,
and promotes community.
It creates a rising tide,
that lifts our Mystic ships, yet again.

Our new embrace is warm and substantial.
Even as our goodbye is sober and heartfelt.
We haven't lost.
We've learned...
and that is ripe fruit for renewal,
and restoration,
and revolution.

Inaugurations and installations,
are both splendid invitations
for a good thing,
a timely thing,
an honorable thing,
even a historic thing...

So have no lamentations in this place.
Our task is both noble and necessary.
We rejoice in what we came to do.
We resound in what we came to do.

We refresh in what we came to do.
We release in what we came to do.

If one holds the torch too long,
the oil of his anointing
will surely burn close and at caution.
Wisdom reproaches and advises,
do not let darkness beckon.
Light a new candle...
and pass it on.

The Centurion awaits her ordination.
The Sentinel watches at the ramparts.
The Vanguard prepares to approach.
The next Herald must have her say.

The same sun shines equally
on antiquity and perpetuity.
Let the old inform the new,
even as the midnight sky
informs the morning dew,
at the break of dawn.
Let what was
become what is,
and is to come.

So let's keep it fresh my friends.
because while the first thing
was a good thing,
a timely thing,
an honorable thing,
even an historic thing...
the next thing matters too.

Let it extend equity.
Let it double down on diversity.

Let it invest in inclusion.
Let it promote community.
Let it create a rising tide,
that lifts our ancient ships, yet again.

Dedicated to Vijaya Sundaram,
Second Poet Laureate of Medford, MA
July 1, 2023

---Afterword---

Brown Skin and the Brilliant Sun is an Opus in the sense that it continues my artistic journey in a series of distinct new movements, extending the threads of faith, love, wonder, conflict, protest, disenchantment, and hope that form the tapestry of my life as a poet and a Christian scribe.

This sixth book doesn't settle things for me. It does, however bring new context and new perspective to many of the themes I've touched on in the first five volumes. I have to talk more about social injustice and racial hatred. I have to talk more about personal pain and human suffering. I have to talk more about how to be in love, faith and community with each other. I have to talk more about Black culture and Black Joy.

This book rings true with the new lessons of tolerance and acceptance that my daughter has taught me. It resonates with the literary power I've gained from being a part of an amazing group of Black Poets Laureate from across the country. And, it is grounded by the loyal support of my wife Terésa, who constantly ministers to me, mind, body and spirit. Her prayers are the milk of human kindness that nourishes our family.

The *Brilliant Sun* makes note of my ancestral connection with the native peoples of this land with a proverb/quote/verse for each chapter heading. I'm exploring this living connection right now. I owe. We all do.

"Like the lines of tree rings, lines on the quahog and whelk shells reflect the movement of the tides over time and amidst men and creatures-aging harmoniously and graciously according to 'the plan of the spirits.'"

Ernestine Gray, Mashpee Wampanoag Artist, Poet, and Musician, 1928-2005

**Terry Eugene Carter, Herald-Poet-Griot
Inaugural Poet Laureate of Medford, MA (2021-2023)
Summer 2023**

Printed in the USA
CPSIA information can be obtained
at www.ICGtesting.com
CBHW021945211023
1443CB00001B/3